The Family Medical Almanac

DR. J FLEETWOOD

Bloomsbury Books · London

To James, Jack, Oliver and Hannah who
weren't even born when my last book, dedicated
to their brothers and sisters, came out

First published by Lochar Publishing Ltd.
Moffat, Scotland DG10 9ED.

This edition published by Bloomsbury Books, an imprint of
The Godfrey Cave Group, 42 Bloomsbury Street, London, WC1B 3QJ,
under licence from Eric Dobby Publishing Ltd,
12 Warnford Road, Orpington, Kent BR6 6LW, 1993

Printed and bound in Great Britain by
BPCC Hazell Books Ltd

Member of BPCC Ltd

ISBN 1 85471 317 5

Contents

PREFACE

The purpose of this book is to summarise in simple terms the principal features of diseases commonly encountered, as well as one or two which could be a hazard further afield. For each condition there is a note on outlook and gravity. The former assumes that adequate treatment is given, for without this even a so-called trivial disease can get out of hand. Gravity is scored on a scale from zero – where there is no threat to health or life – up to four where there is a major risk of serious after affects or even death at five. Where a cross reference is appropriate this appears under the sub-heading 'See also' after 'Gravity rating'. In many cases there are two or more names for the same disease. These may be either technical or popular and appear under 'Alternate name(s)'.

There are a few entries about accident and injury situations for this is a wide subject already very adequately covered in books published by the various First Aid organisations who are always happy to train recruits and the general public in techniques of resuscitation, patient transport and other emergency procedures. For many years I have advocated the teaching of First Aid as a compulsory subject in the final secondary school exams.

No book is ever a purely one-person effort and it is a pleasure to thank those who helped in the preparation of this almanac; in particular our secretary Alison Barnes who prepared the computer print-out and floppy disc and as always my wife for invaluable help in preparing the index and just for being there at crucial moments.

I hope this almanac will supplement the information given to readers by their own doctors, in particular my general practitioner colleagues, who are uniquely placed to give personalised advice to patients whom they have often known for many years.

John Fleetwood MB, FRCGP, DPH, DPA.
Dublin, April 1992

INTRODUCTION

When the publishers and the author came together to discuss the format and contents of this volume in the almanac series one of their first problems was to know what to include. There are literally hundreds of diseases with multiple variations so that simplification into a pocket-sized book is not easy. An old tag says that doctors differ and patients die. Whatever the truth about this there are usually several ways of treating almost any illness and the decision about which to use depends on the doctor in charge who must weigh up numerous factors including the patient's age, sex, general condition, even the social and family situation. We should never forget either that the patient who is bullied or rushed into a treatment for some non-urgent condition is less likely to respond well than one who has been approached as a sensible person entitled to a say in what is to be done for him or her. Five minutes spent explaining procedures to a worried patient or parent are usually well worth while. The days should be long gone when the doctor was regarded as a god in a white coat whose every word was law. Unfortunately the pendulum, as happens so often, has swung to the other extreme and a doctor who has done his or her utmost is blamed because of some unforeseen and unavoidable complication. We should all try to remember that the doctor-patient relationship is a union of allies against the common enemy – disease.

Some of the headings in the present volume, for example, headache and lumbago, refer to symptoms which are common to several possible underlying causes rather than being illnesses in their own right. It is here that accurate diagnosis is vital, for as well as dictating treatment it enables the doctor to make a more accurate estimate of the duration and probable outcome of the illness. A firm diagnosis can sometimes be made on the basis of clinical examination alone. Sometimes laboratory and other tests are necessary, either to confirm a diagnosis or to clarify a doubtful point. It is important to see these tests in proper perspective for they must be regarded as part of an overall examination. Taken in isolation they lose much of their value for apparently identical results may be subject to quite different interpretations in different patients.

There are usually two elements in the treatment of any disease. One is curative and gets at the root of the trouble, while the other aims to restore damage and give general support. In the present volume a good example of this appears under the heading of peritonitis, where the prime treatment is surgical removal of the cause while antibiotics are given to hit any infection present and blood transfusion to correct anaemia due to bleeding so as to give the patient's own body a chance of fighting both infection and shock. This last element is very important for the whole aim of medicine should be to help the body to heal itself, a thing it does with great efficiency if given half a chance and kept in a healthy state by sensible habits, regular exercise, good food and proper living conditions. But of course there are times when even a healthy body needs help and this is where the doctor must try and place his or her shots accurately so as not to injure healthy organs while eliminating disease.

This brings us to one of the great problems encountered in modern medicine. While modern drugs are highly effective many of them produce serious unwanted side-effects to such an extent that patients sometimes wonder whether the treatment is almost worse than the disease. Probably the most marked examples of this are the cytotoxic drugs used to kill cancer cells in malignant tumours. Unfortunately they also effect healthy cells and the sufferer may feel wretched for several days after each treatment. In heart, liver and kidney failure tablets or injections to increase urine output are used. By draining vital minerals, notably potassium, out of the body these drugs can leave a person feeling quite faint and exhausted though here it is relatively easy to relieve the situation either by prescribing potassium (K) tablets or simply by increasing the intake of foods rich in this mineral such as bananas and oranges. With such powerful drugs at our disposal it is more important than ever to take all medicines strictly as ordered by the doctor and not to indulge at the same time in DIY treatment. Even popular, easily available drugs such as headache remedies and stomach mixtures can alter the effects of prescribed treatments, sometimes with disastrous results. For example aspirin will increase the effect of anti-clotting drugs to a level where serious haemorrhages can occur. Women in the early months of pregnancy should be careful about all drugs and are strongly urged to check with their doctor or pharmacist before taking any medications even those bought over the counter outside of pharmacies.

A further point which can cause problems is that an individual may be allergic to particular medicines. Sometimes this allergy results in no more than a transient irritating rash but severe reactions may occur and patients who know of such a personal sensitivity should wear a Medicalert or similar bracelet highlighting this fact in case they are ever treated when unconscious by some doctor unfamiliar with their history.

There is little doubt that viral and bacterial diseases go through varying phases of gravity which have nothing to do with medical advances. Diseases which have been fairly benign may suddenly become aggressive, and vice versa. Sometimes this is related to a community as a whole being debilitated by war, famine and general deprivation, as happened world-wide in 1918 when the Black Flu killed millions of people. We see much the same today in famine - stricken populations of the Third World. Tragically it is usually children who suffer worst in these situations.

Populations can either become relatively immune to common diseases or lose their immunity. There was a striking example of the latter in Hawaii in 1775 when a sailor suffering from measles went ashore and infected the islands where the disease was unknown with the result that 40,000 people out of a population of 150,000 died because they had no natural immunity to what is now a preventable disease. More recently when the inhabitants of Pitcairn Island were evacuated because of danger from a volcano they almost all suffered severe attacks of influenza within days of arriving in the UK. In his novel *The War of the Worlds* H.G. Wells made use of this phenomenon, for the invaders from outer space could not cope with microbes on our planet which were lethal to them, though most of us would be immune. The idea is no longer pure science fiction. Specimens from the moon, and in the not too distant future from other planets must be kept in quarantine in case they harbour infectious germs which might wipe out whole non-immune populations. On the credit side there are diseases which have disappeared, hopefully for ever, and of these smallpox is the most striking example. No cases of this highly infectious condition have been reported anywhere for over a decade.

Sometimes both practising doctors and back-room investigators can often claim that they have made a positive impact on a disease. Fifty years ago puerperal sepsis and pneumonia were potential killers with a high mortality rate. The discovery of sulphonamides, penicillin and the many other antibiotics which followed changed the picture for ever. Unfortunately some germs have developed resistance to antibiotics so that there is a constant search for new and more effective ones.

There is no doubt that diseases and diagnoses go through fashions. There used to be a great vogue for what was called a 'spastic colon'. Nowadays we talk of the 'irritable bowel syndrome' which will probably give way to some other name tag in the future.

Every now and again we read of what seem to be new diseases and we ask ourselves: 'Was this disease always present in a less virulent form or is it due to some mutation of a germ caused by radiation, pollution or an unknown factor?' Fifteen years ago a popular encyclopaedia of medicine did not even mention AIDS, now one of the most sinister health threats ever to confront humanity. Why this sudden spread? No one really knows.

A factor in the spread of infectious diseases from one country or continent to another is air travel. When journeys took weeks or even months to complete on board ships these diseases could incubate and declare themselves. Nowadays with no part of the world more than 48 hours away from anywhere else it is all too easy for people incubating a disease to be infecting others thousands of miles from their country of origin. Up to the beginning of this century, ships and passengers from 'suspect' areas were placed in quarantine but this is just not feasible at a twentieth-century airport where tens of thousands of passengers pass through every hour.

Fortunately it is now possible to vaccinate travellers against many diseases likely to be encountered abroad. Typhoid, plague, typhus, cholera, rabies, yellow fever and malaria are still common in many undeveloped countries. There are vaccines available for the first six but no matter what injections, or in the case of malaria tablets, are given travellers should exercise common sense and be careful of what or where they eat or drink in countries where sanitation takes a low priority.

Nearer home more and more infectious diseases are becoming preventable. Measles, mumps, whooping cough, rubella, poliomyelitis, tetanus and diphtheria can all be prevented by prophylactic injections. There is even work being done which gives hope that it may be possible to vaccinate against certain types of cancer. But a lot remains to be done. If only the billions spent on destruction could be channelled into research, the provision of clean water and universal hygiene measures what a lovely, healthy world we could have.

The speed of medical advances is sometimes breathtaking. In the body of the text for example it is stated that there is no cure for AIDS. While regretfully this is still true, since it was written only a few months ago several promising lines of treatment have developed and hopefully one or more of these will lead to a real cure in the not too distant future.

First Aid

Properly applied first aid has saved countless lives. Unfortunately inefficient methods can make injuries worse or even cause death. The brief notes which follow are for guidance only and readers are strongly urged to enrol with one of the first aid organisations for a training course where they will have an opportunity to ask questions and get practical experience in resuscitation, bandaging, patient transport and other procedures.

Many accidents, particularly in the home, could be avoided. Faulty electrical and gas fittings, slippery floors, careless storage of medicines, household cleansers and inflammable liquids, shaky bannisters, worn carpets and unguarded fires have all caused injury and death. Prevention is always better than cure.

If a serious accident happens and you know what to do, can you or someone else summon further help quickly? Write down these emergency telephone numbers for your area now;

Doctor _____

Ambulance _____

Fire Brigade _____

Poisons Centre _____

Police _____

Very often the simplest first aid is the best and all that is sometimes needed is to make the victim comfortable, reassure him or her and send for more expert help. There are three situations where **IMMEDIATE** help by whoever is at hand is essential if a life is to be saved. They are choking, asphyxia and severe bleeding (haemorrhage).

CHOKING

Choking is due to an obstructed airway. The situation is usually obvious. The victim starts gasping and cannot speak after gulping down unchewed food or a child puts some small object in its mouth and sucks it back. Within seconds the face becomes white and then blue. Quick removal of the obstruction is essential. With great luck it may be possible to get hold of some projection from the inhaled object and pull it out. Children often put medium sized balls into their mouths and here, of course, there is nothing to grasp. Sometimes one can hook an obstruction out of the mouth with the handle of a small spoon. On no account should a standing or sitting child be slapped on the back. The only result will be to cause it to gasp and draw the obstruction further in and if this cannot be removed easily within seconds then the Heimlich manoeuvre must be used. The object is to force air up from the victim's lungs through the airways with sufficient force to expel almost any foreign body. There are four steps;

1. Stand behind the patient holding them around the torso between the navel and the lower ribs.
2. Try to get them to lean forward limply.
3. Make a fist of your right hand. Place it a couple of inches below the lower tip of the breastbone. Grasp the fist with your left hand.
4. Exert sudden, strong, upwards and inwards pressure against the sufferer's abdomen. Do not squeeze the ribs. Repeat several times if necessary until the obstruction is expelled sometimes with considerable force.

If the person is lying or sitting the manoeuvre can still be carried out quite effectively. In a child the pressure applied should be less than for a muscular adult. Quite a number of people have saved their own lives by using this manoeuvre when there is no one else around to help.

ASPHYXIA

Asphyxia causes death in choking but may also follow inhalation of fumes or smoke, immersion in water or external obstruction to breathing. One's whole instinct in the first two is to dash into what may be a very dangerous atmosphere in a heroic rescue attempt. Do three things first which only take a few seconds;

1. Raise the alarm.
2. Wedge the door open.
3. Take several deep breaths of good air.

Then go in holding your breath and if smoke is the problem keep as close to the floor as possible. Drag the person into clean air. If the person is breathing simply observe while waiting for an ambulance. Turn them on their side and be prepared to clear the mouth if they vomit. If they are not breathing check that there is no obstruction such as a dental plate in the mouth and start resuscitation;

1. Lift the chin and tilt the head well back.
2. Pinch the nostrils between your thumb and fore-finger.
3. Take a deep breath.
4. Place your mouth over the victim's mouth (over the mouth and nose for a small child) and blow firmly once every five seconds.
5. Watch the victim's chest. It should rise and fall in time with your breathing.
6. If there is no rise recheck the mouth and tilt the head further back.
7. Continue until the person breathes without assistance or until a doctor confirms death.

If the asphyxia is due to smoke and the clothes are on fire these must, of course, be extinguished first by smothering the flames with a fire blanket which should be standard equipment in every kitchen, workshop or anywhere with a fire hazard including motor cars. Failing a proper blanket a coat, sacking or similar material can be used.

HAEMORRHAGE

Severe bleeding is usually due to injury involving either a vein or an artery. Direct, firm, continued pressure with a clean pad will stop most bleeding and once this has been done the immediate emergency is under control. The patient should be put in a comfortable position with the bleeding area uppermost. Pressure must be maintained until a doctor is available.

The three conditions described above are all life threatening requiring quick positive action. For those listed alphabetically below simple first aid is usually the best. The golden rules are;

1. Treat the obvious injury.
2. Do a quick check for further injuries.
3. Unless there is grave danger or the injury is obviously trivial do not move the person.
4. Never try to force liquid into an unconscious person's mouth.
5. Treat for shock by rest and warmth.
6. Keep calm and do not alarm the patient.

BRUISING

This is bleeding which has not come out. While it rarely constitutes a serious emergency it may indicate an underlying fracture or oozing loss of blood from an internal organ. If pain is severe and movement makes it worse assume that a fracture is present until proved otherwise usually by X-ray. For minor bruising apply cold packs and keep the part at rest. If there is no suspicion of a more serious underlying injury hot packs may be applied twenty four hours later to help the bruise dissolve.

BURNS

Heat, cold and chemicals all cause burns. For major heat burns put the patient at rest, cover the area with clean cloth such as freshly laundered sheets, handkerchiefs etc., which may be either dry or soaked in boiled water to which common salt has been added in the proportion of one teaspoonful of salt to a pint of water. This would only be worth while if there is likely to be a long delay in transfer to hospital when in addition simple pain killing drugs such as aspirin should be given with drinks of warm, sweet tea. For minor burns immerse the burned part at once in cold water, dry gently and apply a clean dressing. For both major and minor burns **DO NOT;**

Pull off clothing which has stuck to the skin.
Try to open blisters.
Apply anaesthetic sprays, butter or any cream which could be contaminated.

Burns due to intense cold should be treated in the same way except that cold packs should not be used. For chemical burns wash off corrosive liquid with clean water then treat as for a heat burn. If corrosive liquids get into the eyes or mouth use plenty of water to wash away as much as possible. Cover the eye with a clean pad and in both cases seek medical aid quickly.

CHILDBIRTH

This may be premature or full term. In unexpected labour the delivery is usually quick and straightforward. If there is time spread a proofed material such as plastic covered with a clean sheet over the bed. When the woman is lying down remove any underclothing which could obstruct expulsion of the baby. If there is time boil a scissors, a couple of strips of bandage or tape and some cotton wool. Make sure that these have cooled before using them. If a disinfectant is available put some into the water. Wash your hands thoroughly and clean the birth area with the boiled cotton wool. Make no attempt to either hinder or help the delivery. Leave it to nature. As the baby's head is born support it and be ready for the rest of the body to follow. When the womb contracts (labour pains) and the head is born very gentle easing out of the baby may help. Do not put any tension on the umbilical cord at any time. Clean the baby's mouth with gauze or cotton wool. Do not try to clean its body which will be very slippery. Place the baby face down on the mother's abdomen and if it does not breath within a couple of minutes hold it head down by the legs and either put a cotton wool pad soaked in cold water between the shoulders or pat it gently in the same area. If this does not succeed do gentle mouth-to-mouth breathing as described above for asphyxia. When the baby breathes tie two pieces of boiled bandage or tape firmly around the umbilical cord about five and seven inches from the navel. Cut the cord between the tapes and give the baby to the mother. The afterbirth or placenta should be delivered within a few minutes. Gentle massaging of the abdomen will help this. Never pull on the umbilical cord. Keep the mother comfortable and give her a cup of tea or coffee.

ELECTRICAL INJURIES

It cannot be emphasised too strongly that the vast majority of electrical accidents could be avoided by following four simple rules;

1. Only purchase appliances with a recognised safety rating.
2. Ensure that even the simplest electrical installation is correctly carried out.
3. Maintain equipment properly.
4. Insist that safe practices are followed both in the work place and at home.

If an accident does occur injury can range from trivial burns to death. Severe burns and broken bones due to violent muscular contraction occur in a considerable number of cases.

Before touching the victim the source of supply must be cut off. Otherwise the rescuer may also be electrocuted. Switching off may not be adequate if a short circuit has occurred and unplugging if possible is preferable. Where a bare wire is in contact with the person this should either be cut with an **insulated** wire cutter or hatchet. If no proper tool is available then the wire may be pulled or pushed clear with some non-conductor such as a **dry** rope or wooden pole.

If the person is not breathing the Kiss-of-Life must be commenced immediately as described under Asphyxia. Burns and fractures should be treated as appropriate and if there is any doubt about more serious injuries then the patient should be taken to hospital.

Children are particularly at risk in the home where light sockets and power points must never be accessible to little fingers. Child-proof protective covers should be routinely fitted. Stress to older children that daring each other to climb electric pylons or protective fences around sub-stations is just plain stupid and never let anyone of any age bring a mains radio or television into the bathroom. Electricity and water make a lethal combination.

EPILEPTIC SEIZURE

There may be a few seconds warning during which the person can be put lying sideways on the floor in a safe spot e.g. away from fire or passing traffic. Never force the mouth open but if the jaw relaxes of its own accord then put in a wad of paper or some similar firm but not brittle material between the teeth. If vomiting occurs clear out the mouth. If breathing stops be prepared to do mouth-to-mouth resuscitation.

FLESH WOUNDS

Clean the area with soap and water or a mild antiseptic. Put on a clean pad and bandage firmly. If the wound is penetrating e.g. from a dog bite or a pointed instrument then the possibility of a deeper injury or later tetanus should be remembered and medical advice obtained.

FOREIGN BODIES (FBs)

This usually applies to small objects being stuck in the eye, ear or nose very often by a child. In the eye if the FB is small it may be possible to lift it out with a swab or wash it out with an eye lotion. No more than two attempts should be made and if these fail the eye should be covered and medical help sought. In the ear no effort should be made to remove an impacted pea, bead or similar object. This is a matter for skilled care. Blowing the nose hard while pressing the other nostril firmly will often dislodge a small FB.

FRACTURES

Any break in a bone either small or large is a fracture. There is usually a history of some violence either accidental or deliberate. There is always pain and in the case of a large bone the snap as it breaks may be heard. The break should be immobilised by the use of a splint, sling or other support before the patient is moved. If the bone protrudes through the skin (compound fracture) the wound should be covered or bandaged firmly enough to control bleeding but not so tightly as to cause pain.

A patient with a possible fracture of the backbone should never be moved except by an experienced team using proper equipment. The condition should be suspected after a severe fall if there is either numbness or severe pain in the arms or legs. This may be due to pressure on the spinal cord and this is where unskilled treatment and movement could result in permanent paralysis below the level of the break. Just keep the patient comfortable and wait unless you have been trained.

Similarly a skull fracture should be suspected after a fall if the patient is dizzy, vomiting, dazed, seeing double or unconscious even for a couple of seconds. A bleeding wound in the head makes the diagnosis even more possible. The victim should be kept resting until he or she has been examined by a doctor. If there is a strong smell of alcohol it does not exclude a fractured skull complicating a drunken stupor. Always hope for the best but treat for the worst.

FROSTBITE

This is due to overexposure to temperature low enough to cause part of the body to freeze. The feet, hands, nose and ears are particularly at risk. Tingling is the first symptom, followed by numbness and if the condition is neglected gangrene. In early cases the part should be immersed if possible in warm (not hot) water. Non-alcoholic drinks are given and the patient kept warm with extra clothing and protection from wind. As feeling returns he or she should be encouraged to wriggle the fingers and toes. In more severe cases admission to hospital will be necessary. In all cases there are several **DON'TS** to be observed. Never rub the affected part vigorously. Never put hot jars against the frozen area. The victim should never sit or lie too close to a fire, radiator or heat lamp.

Every year mountain rescue teams have to deal with cases of exposure and frost bite because people go into the Highlands in winter with inadequate clothing. Boots should be strong and waterproof. Spare stockings should be carried in an inside pocket and put on if the feet get wet. Mittens are preferable to gloves and outer clothing should be loose, warm and both wind and water proof. A hooded Inverness cape is an excellent outer garment for wear in even the harshest conditions

HEATSTROKE

This follows excessive sweating, failure of which is a very serious complication. After initial flushing and sweating the skin becomes clammy and pale. The sufferer feels faint and often nauseated. If unattended the temperature rises to dangerous levels. Take the following steps quickly;

1. Get the person into the coolest, shaded area possible.
2. Cool the body by sponging with cold water.
3. If able to swallow give a glass of water or tomato juice with a teaspoonful of salt. Do not gulp this down. Sip slowly.
4. Call an ambulance.

POISONING

If poison has been swallowed and the person complains of severe burning in the mouth and throat the mouth should be washed out several times with plain water and then a pint of water swallowed. Anything vomited up and the vessel containing the poison should be kept for further examination. The nearest poisons centre should be contacted and medical aid sought.

SHOCK

Shock may develop after what appears to be a trivial injury and should be anticipated in any major accident. The best steps to take are;

1. Put the patient lying down with the head lower than the rest of the body.
2. Control bleeding.
3. Watch breathing and check the pulse frequently for changes in rate, irregularity or weakness.
4. Keep the patient comfortably warm.
5. If conscious and no likelihood of an internal injury give warm, sweet tea. **DO NOT** give alcohol.

SPRAIN

This is a pulling injury to the supports around a joint. First aid includes rest, support and cold compresses to the area. An elastic non-adhesive bandage applied firmly but not too tightly gives excellent support. Pain persisting for more than twenty four hours suggests that a fracture may be present requiring X-ray examination for confirmation.

Every home and every motor car should contain a simple first aid kit. Most pharmacies have these ready made up. They cost very little and could save a lot of distress. But always remember that prevention is better than cure.

The Human
Body

The Skeleton

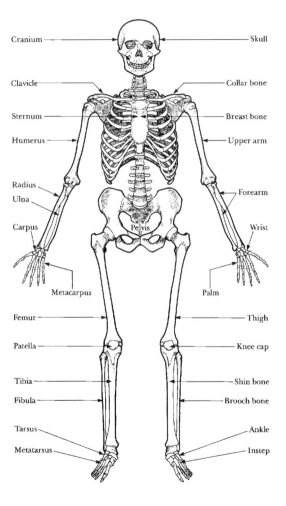

Cranium — Skull

Clavicle — Collar bone

Sternum — Breast bone

Humerus — Upper arm

Radius —
Ulna — Forearm

Carpus —
Pelvis — Wrist

Metacarpus — Palm

Femur — Thigh

Patella — Knee cap

Tibia — Shin bone

Fibula — Brooch bone

Tarsus — Ankle

Metatarsus — Instep

Outline of Thoracic and Abdominal Organs

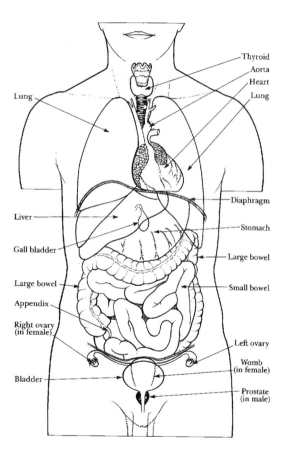

Thyroid
Aorta
Heart
Lung

Lung

Diaphragm

Liver

Stomach

Gall bladder

Large bowel

Large bowel

Small bowel

Appendix

Right ovary
(in female)

Left ovary

Womb
(in female)

Bladder

Prostate
(in male)

The Upper Abdomen

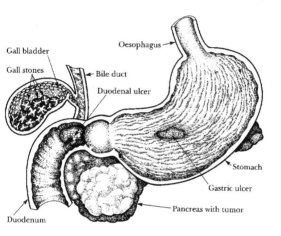

Oesophagus

Gall bladder

Gall stones

Bile duct

Duodenal ulcer

Stomach

Gastric ulcer

Pancreas with tumor

Duodenum

The Chest Cavity
(Thorax)

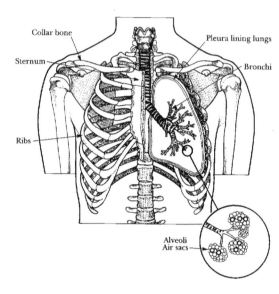

Collar bone

Pleura lining lungs

Sternum

Bronchi

Ribs

Alveoli
Air sacs

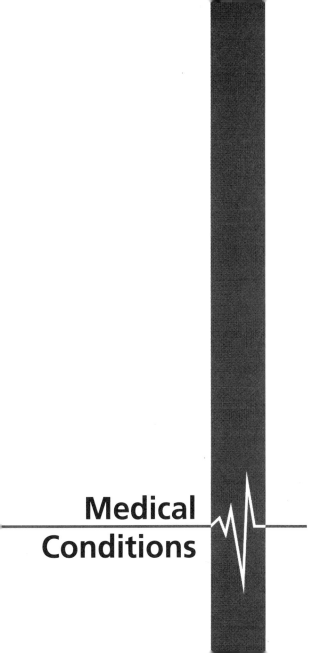

Medical
Conditions

Common name:	**ABORTION**
Alternate name(s):	Early miscarriage.
Cause:	May follow injury, illness, over-exertion, unknown, hormone deficiency.
Early symptoms:	Abdominal cramps.
Course:	Bleeding, loss of embryo.
Complications:	Severe bleeding, infection, sterility, depression.
Treatment:	Rest, sedatives, operation, counselling.
Outlook:	Good.
Prevention:	Regular pre-natal care.
Gravity rating 2	

Common name:	**ABSCESS (External)**
Alternate name(s):	Furuncle, folliculitis, boil.
Cause:	Bacteria entering a small skin break.
Early symptoms:	Redness, slight pain.
Course:	Local swelling, more severe pain.
Complications:	General spread, septicaemia.
Treatment:	Antibiotics, local dressings, lancing.
Outlook:	Good.
Prevention:	Clean small injuries.
Gravity rating 1:	See also boils, carbuncles, septicaemia.

Common name:	**ABSCESS (Internal)**
Alternate name(s):	Not appropriate.
Cause:	Infection of an internal organ.
Early symptoms:	Pain, shivering, temperature.
Course:	Severe upset, high temperature, collapse.
Complications:	Blood poisoning, peritonitis, infection in a vital area.
Treatment:	Antibiotics, surgery.
Outlook:	Fair.
Prevention:	Early treatment of any infection.
Gravity rating 2:	See also septicaemia.

Common Name:	**ACNE**
Alternate name(s):	Not appropriate.
Cause:	Blockage of skin glands by sweat.
Early symptoms:	Blackheads appearing on skin.
Course:	Enlargement of blocked ducts.
Complications:	Infection, scarring.
Treatment:	Hygiene of skin, low-fat type of diet, UV light, drainage, hormone treatment, antibiotics.
Outlook:	Good.
Prevention:	Skin hygiene, avoidance of fatty foods.
Gravity rating 0:	See also seborrhoea.

Common Name:	**ACTINOMYCOSIS**
Alternate name(s):	Lumpy jaw.
Cause:	Fungus infection.
Early symptoms:	Swelling around jaws.
Course:	Skin is locally destroyed.
Complications:	Generalised spread.
Treatment:	Antibiotics, drainage of abscesses, X-ray therapy.
Outlook:	Good.
Prevention:	Hygiene, particularly on farms.

Gravity rating 2

Common name:	**ADDISON'S DISEASE**
Alternate name(s):	Adrenal hypofunction.
Cause:	Infection (often tubercular) of adrenal glands.
Early symptoms:	Tiredness, skin darkens.
Course:	Weight loss, nausea, fall of blood pressure, reduced resistance to infections.
Complications:	Reduced resistance to infections, mental changes.
Treatment:	Replacement of deficient hormone, control of exercise and diet.
Outlook:	Poor.
Prevention:	Treatment of TB infection elsewhere.
Gravity rating 4:	See also blood pressure (low).

Common name: **ADENOIDS**
Alternate name(s): Adenoid hyperplasia, chronic adenoiditis.
Cause: Chronic infection of back of nose.
Early symptoms: Nasal obstruction, snoring, catarrh.
Course: Chronic infection.
Complications: Ear infections.
Treatment: Antibiotics, surgery.
Outlook: Good.
Prevention: Not appropriate.
Gravity rating 1

Common name: **AIDS**
Alternate name(s): Acquired Immune Deficiency Syndrome, HIV infection.
Cause: Infection with human immune deficiency virus by sexual contact, contaminated blood transfusion. Sometimes by infected blood, semen or other body fluids coming in contact with an open cut or sore.
Early symptoms: General malaise, swollen glands, diarrhoea, fever.
Course: Progressive deterioration and multiple infections.
Complications: Pneumonia, Kaposi's sarcoma.
Treatment: None known at present. Symptomatic. Social and psychological support.
Outlook: Poor.
Prevention: Avoid infected sexual partners and communal syringes, use condoms.
Gravity rating 5: See also syphilis, gonorrhoea, herpes.

Common name:	**ALLERGY**
Alternate name(s):	Hypersensitivity.
Cause:	Reaction to substances such as pollen, food, drugs, animal dander.
Early symptoms:	Sneezing, lachrimation, rash, itching.
Course:	Asthma, eczema in some cases.
Complications:	Shock, collapse, choking.
Treatment:	Anti-allergy tablets, liquids, injections, steroids.
Outlook:	Variable.
Prevention:	Avoid known allergens.
Gravity rating 3:	See also hay fever, hives, asthma, migraine, eczema.

Common name:	**ALZHEIMER'S DISEASE**
Alternate name(s):	Pre-senile dementia, the 'living death'.
Cause:	Degeneration of blood supply to brain.
Early symptoms:	Minor confusion.
Course:	Increasing confusion, memory failure, incontinence.
Complications:	Injury due to failure to appreciate environmental dangers.
Treatment:	Supportive, social services.
Outlook:	Progressive deterioration.
Prevention:	None known.
Gravity rating 4	

Common name:	**AMENORRHOEA**
Alternate name(s):	Absence of periods.
Cause:	Malnutrition, from whatever cause including anorexia nervosa, anaemia, hormone defect, stress, pregnancy.
Early symptoms:	Intermittent or sudden cessation of periods.
Course:	Not appropriate.
Complications:	Not appropriate.
Treatment:	Correction of cause.
Outlook:	Good.
Prevention:	Not appropriate.

Gravity rating 1

Common name:	**ANAEMIA**
Alternate name(s):	Bloodlessness.
Cause:	Two main groups. 1. Blood loss, destruction of red cells, failure to form new cells. 2. Nutritional disorders.
Early symptoms:	Fatigue, pallor.
Course:	Numbness, tingling of hands and feet, exhaustion, loss of breath, fast pulse, confusion.
Complications:	Damage to nerves, heart and brain.
Treatment:	Find and eliminate cause. Iron, vitamin B12, folic acid, blood transfusion.
Outlook:	Variable.
Prevention:	Check possible sources of bleeding, diet.

Gravity rating 3

Common name:	**ANEURYSM**
Alternate name(s):	Bulging artery.
Cause:	Chronic infection, injury, hardening.
Early symptoms:	Discomfort in area of vessel.
Course:	Pain, swelling, brain symptoms if in brain.
Complications:	Rupture, bleeding, symptoms related to area supplied.
Treatment:	Surgical.
Outlook:	Progressive.
Prevention:	None.
Gravity rating 3:	See also subarachnoid haemorrhage.

Common name:	**ANGINA PECTORIS**
Alternate name(s):	Coronary pain.
Cause:	Spasm of coronary artery.
Early symptoms:	Tight chest feeling on exertion.
Course:	More severe pain on less exertion.
Complications:	Blockage of coronary artery.
Treatment:	Anti-spasmodic drugs, by-pass surgery, surgical dilatation.
Outlook:	Fair.
Prevention:	Stop smoking, reduce weight, regular exercise, lower cholesterol, relieve stress.
Gravity rating 4:	See also arterio-sclerosis, coronary thrombosis, blood pressure, heart failure.

Common name: **ANOREXIA NERVOSA**
Alternate name(s): Slimmer's disease.
Cause: Variable, psychosis.
Early symptoms: Reduced intake of food and excessive exercising.
Course: Self-induced vomiting, gross weight loss.
Complications: Psychotic and neurotic symptoms, loss of energy, suicide.
Treatment: Psychotherapy, family counselling.
Outlook: Poor.
Prevention: None known.
Gravity rating 3: See also depression.

Common name: **APHTHOUS ULCER**
Alternate name(s): Mouth ulcer.
Cause: Possible allergy.
Early symptoms: Small painful ulcer in mouth.
Course: Heals in ten days.
Complications: Infection, malnutrition.
Treatment: Mouth hygiene, local anaesthetic tablets, local steroid.
Outlook: Good.
Prevention: Regular dental care.
Gravity rating 0

Common name: **APPENDICITIS**
Alternate name(s): Not appropriate.
Cause: Infection of appendix.
Early symptoms: Mid-abdominal pain, nausea.
Course: Pain moves to right side, vomiting, slight temperature.
Complications: Rupture of appendix, peritonitis.
Treatment: Surgery, antibiotics.
Outlook: Good.
Prevention: None known.
Gravity rating 1

Common name: **ARTERIO-SCLEROSIS**
Alternate name(s): Arterial hardening.
Cause: Many factors including diet, heredity, diabetes, gout.
Early symptoms: Depend on location.
Limbs: cold numb extremities, cramps.
Heart: angina pectoris.
Brain: confusion.
Course: Increase of symptoms.
Complications: Gangrene, heart attack, senile state, stroke.
Treatment: By-pass surgery, drugs to reduce clotting, lower cholesterol, stop smoking.
Outlook: Poor.
Prevention: Removal or reduction of identifiable factors.
Gravity rating 4: See also angina pectoris, Buerger's disease, gangrene.

Common name:	**ARTHRITIS**
Alternate name(s):	Joint inflammation.
Cause:	Injury, infection.
Early symptoms:	Pain, stiffness.
Course:	Pain and disability become more severe.
Complications:	Joint may become locked.
Treatment:	Heat, rest, anti-inflammatory drugs, physiotherapy.
Outlook:	Good.
Prevention:	Treat minor injuries of joints with care.
Gravity rating 2:	See also rheumatism, rheumatoid arthritis, osteoarthritis, gout.

Common name:	**ASCITES**
Alternate name(s):	Dropsy, fluid in abdomen.
Cause:	Heart or kidney failure, internal growths, liver cirrhosis.
Early symptoms:	Breathlessness, abdominal discomfort.
Course:	Swollen abdomen.
Complications:	Pressure on internal organs.
Treatment:	Treat cause, surgical removal of fluid, increase urine flow.
Outlook:	Poor.
Prevention:	Early treatment of cause.
Gravity rating 4:	See also heart failure, nephritis, cirrhosis.

Common name:	**ASTHMA**
Alternate name(s):	Bronchospasm.
Cause:	Often allergic, stress.
Early symptoms:	Breathlessness.
Course:	Severe breathlessness, wheezing, distress.
Complications:	Acute heart and lung failure.
Treatment:	Tablets, fluids, inhalers, injections to relieve attacks, steroids, oxygen, anti-allergy drugs.
Outlook:	Poor.
Prevention:	Early treatment of cause. Avoid known triggers.
Gravity rating 4:	See also allergy.

Common name:	**ATHLETE'S FOOT**
Alternate name(s):	Tinea pedis.
Cause:	Fungal infection.
Early symptoms:	Itching, scaling, foul smell from foot.
Course:	Cracking of skin, secondary infection.
Complications:	Spread of infection.
Treatment:	Hygiene with anti-fungal creams.
Outlook:	Good.
Prevention:	Avoid barefoot walking in changing rooms.
Gravity rating 0:	See also ringworm.

Common name:	**AUTISM**
Alternate name(s):	Not appropriate.
Cause:	Unknown.
Early symptoms:	Over-reaction to new situations, anger, rage.
Course:	Major social difficulties, withdrawn.
Complications:	Severe learning problems.
Treatment:	Sedation, special education.
Outlook:	Poor.
Prevention:	None known.
Gravity rating 3:	See also schizophrenia.

Common name:	**BEDSORES**
Alternate name(s):	Decubitus ulcers, pressure sores.
Cause:	Lying in one position too long in wet or soiled bed.
Early symptoms:	Skin reddens over pressure areas.
Course:	Skin is locally destroyed.
Complications:	Infection.
Treatment:	Clean area, relieve pressure, change position.
Outlook:	Fair.
Prevention:	Frequent position change, hygiene, good nutrition.
Gravity rating 2:	See also gangrene.

Common name:	**BELL'S PALSY**
Alternate name(s):	Facial paralysis, 7th cranial nerve palsy.
Cause:	Local chilling, injury, tumour.
Early symptoms:	Pain behind and under ear.
Course:	Eye remains open, mouth pulled to one side, dribbling, loss of taste sense.
Complications:	Permanent paralysis, facial distortion, eye infection.
Treatment:	Removal of cause, splinting lip, physiotherapy, cosmetic surgery, steroids, pain relief.
Outlook:	Good.
Prevention:	Avoid draughts on back of ear.
Gravity rating 1:	See also neuritis.

Common name:	**BLEPHARITIS**
Alternate name(s):	Not appropriate.
Cause:	Eyelid infection.
Early symptoms:	Itching, burning, swollen eyelid(s).
Course:	Blisters and pus formation, lids stick together.
Complications:	Distortion of eyelids.
Treatment:	Local antibiotics.
Outlook:	Good.
Prevention:	Hygiene.
Gravity rating 1:	See also stye, conjunctivitis, trachoma.

Common name:	**BLOOD PRESSURE (HIGH)**
Alternate name(s):	Hypertension.
Cause:	Often unknown, kidney disease, arteriosclerosis, stress.
Early symptoms:	Varied, headaches, blurred vision.
Course:	Nausea and vomiting, vertigo.
Complications:	Heart failure, angina pectoris, coronary disease, kidney failure, stroke.
Treatment:	Anti-hypertensive drugs, treatment of cause if known, adjustment of life style.
Outlook:	Fair.
Prevention:	Regular measurement of pressure, treatment of kidney disease.
Gravity rating 4:	See also coronary disease, arterio-sclerosis, nephritis.

Common name:	**BLOOD PRESSURE (LOW)**
Alternate name(s):	Hypotension.
Cause:	Infection of adrenal glands, diabetic coma, shock, unknown.
Early symptoms:	Tiredness, vertigo on standing up.
Course:	Faintness, collapse.
Complications:	Injury on falling.
Treatment:	Treat cause, change posture slowly to avoid blackouts.
Outlook:	Fair.
Prevention:	Change posture slowly to avoid blackouts.
Gravity rating 2:	see also Addison's disease, fainting.

Common name:	**BRONCHIECTASIS**
Alternate name(s):	Chronic lung infection.
Cause:	Repeated neglected chest infections.
Early symptoms:	Recurrent bouts of coughing, dirty sputum.
Course:	Coughing of blood, severe breathlessness, fever, fatigue.
Complications:	Pneumonia, emphysema.
Treatment:	Removal of septic teeth and tonsils. Long term anti-biotics, expectorants. Drainage.
Outlook:	Fair.
Prevention:	Prompt care of respiratory infections.
Gravity rating 4:	See also bronchitis, emphysema, pneumonia.

Common name:	**BRONCHITIS**
Alternate name(s):	Not appropriate.
Cause:	Viral or bacterial infection of lungs.
Early symptoms:	Cough, chest discomfort, slight temperature.
Course:	Clear or coloured sputum, cough.
Complications:	Pneumonia, emphysema, bronchiectasis.
Treatment:	Rest, inhalations, cough mixture, antibiotics.
Outlook:	Good.
Prevention:	Prompt treatment of colds, avoid smoking and irritants.
Gravity rating 2:	See also bronchiectasis, pneumonia.

Common name:	**BRUCELLOSIS**
Alternate name(s):	Undulant fever.
Cause:	Infection from cattle and other animals.
Early symptoms:	Slight fever, headaches, fatigue, bone pains.
Course:	Enlargement of glands, spleen, liver.
Complications:	Haemorrhages, heart, liver involvment, neuritis.
Treatment:	Antibiotics.
Outlook:	Fair.
Prevention:	Eradication of brucellosis in animals.

Gravity rating 3

Common name:	**BUERGER'S DISEASE**
Alternate name(s):	Thromboangiitis obliterans.
Cause:	Blockage of small blood vessels in legs.
Early symptoms:	Numbness, coldness, tingling of legs on exertion.
Course:	Cramps, continuous symptoms even at rest.
Complications:	Severe pain, clotting, gangrene, angina, eye damage.
Treatment:	Avoid all smoking, temperature extremes, prompt care of injuries, graduated exercises, anti-clotting drugs, by-pass surgery, amputation.
Outlook:	Fair.
Prevention:	Avoid smoking, lose weight if necessary.
Gravity rating 4:	See also arterio-sclerosis, gangrene.

Common name:	**BUNION**
Alternate name(s):	Bursitis of big toe.
Cause:	Pressure.
Early symptoms:	Pain, limping.
Course:	Distortion of toe.
Complications:	Infection of underlying bone.
Treatment:	Surgery after clearing inflammation.
Outlook:	Good.
Prevention:	Proper footwear.
Gravity rating 0:	See also bursitis.

Common name:	**BURSITIS**
Alternate name(s):	Periarticular inflammation.
Cause:	Inflammation of padding around a joint.
Early symptoms:	Pain and tenderness.
Course:	Stiffness.
Complications:	Becoming chronic, septic infection.
Treatment:	Rest, anti-inflammatory drugs, physiotherapy.
Outlook:	Good.
Prevention:	Avoid sudden strains and chronic pressure.
Gravity rating 1:	See also arthritis, synovitis.

Common name:	**CAISSON DISEASE**
Alternate name(s):	The bends, diver's paralysis.
Cause:	Sudden decompression releases nitrogen bubbles into blood.
Early symptoms:	Feeling of pressure, nausea.
Course:	Severe joint pains, paralysis.
Complications:	Permanent nerve damage.
Treatment:	Compression chamber, gradual decompression.
Outlook:	Fair.
Prevention:	Slow decompression after deep diving.

Gravity rating 3

Common name:	**CANCER**
Alternate name(s):	Malignancy, neoplasm, tumour, growth, carcinoma, sarcoma.
Cause:	Often unknown, chronic irritation, radiation, smoking, chemicals.
Early symptoms:	Cancer may attack any organ. Early diagnosis is vital.
Course:	The chart shows symptoms and signs which should always be medically investigated.
Treatment:	Surgery, radiation, hormones, cytotoxic drugs, steroids, cryosurgery.
Outlook:	Variable.
Prevention:	Avoid proven cancer-producing situations and substances.
Gravity rating 4:	See also leukaemia, Hodgkin's disease, myeloma.

POSSIBLE WARNING SIGNS

Bladder: Increasing frequency of urination. Pain passing water. Blood in urine.

Breast: Lump. Nipple becoming distorted or turned inwards. Lumps in the armpit. Discharge from nipple.

Kidney: Increasing frequency of urination. Blood in urine. Dull pain in loins.

Leukaemia: Tiredness. Loss of weight. Swollen glands. Pain in bones. Poor appetite. Recurrent sore throats.

Lower Bowel: Full feeling in bowel after passing motion. Blood and mucus in stool. Alternating constipation and diarrhoea. Excess flatus. Change in normal bowel pattern. Recurring cramps in abdomen. Swelling of abdomen.

Lung: Persistent cough in a heavy smoker. Bloodstained sputum. Recurrent pneumonia. Chest pain.

Mouth & Tongue: Sore that does not heal.

Oesophagus: Difficulty in swallowing. Foul odour from breath. Feeling of obstruction behind the breastbone. Regurgitation of food.

Prostate: Difficulty in passing water. Blood in urine.

Skin: Change in mole or wart. Failure of small sore to heal.

Stomach: Indigestion. Nausea. Black 'tarry' bowel motions.

Throat: Persistent hoarseness. Bloodstained sputum.

Womb: Bleeding or discharge from the vagina between periods or after change of life. Bleeding after intercourse.

Common name: **CANDIDIASIS**
Alternate name(s): Thrush, monilial infection.
Cause: Fungus infection.

A) CANDIDIASIS (MOUTH)

Early symptoms: Soreness.
Course: White patches.
Complications: Spread, secondary infection.
Treatment: Mouth hygiene, anti-fungal mouthwash.
Outlook: Good.
Prevention: Personal hygiene preparing and consuming food, improve nutrition.

Gravity rating 1

B) CANDIDIASIS (VAGINA)

Early symptoms: Intense itching.
Course: Discharge.
Complications: Secondary infection, recurrence.
Treatment: Personal hygiene, anti-fungal pessaries or cream, treat sexual partner.
Outlook: Fair.
Prevention: Personal hygiene, avoid sex with infected partner.

Gravity rating 2

C) CANDIDIASIS (SKIN)

Early symptoms: Soreness especially between toes, under breasts, warm moist areas.
Course: Not appropriate.
Complications: Secondary infection.
Treatment: Skin hygiene, avoid tight clothing, anti-fungal powder.
Outlook: Good.

Prevention:	Frequent clothing change, personal hygiene, anti-fungal powder in socks.

Gravity rating 1

D) CANDIDIASIS (BOWEL)

Cause:	May follow antibiotic treatment or use of contraceptive pill.
Early symptoms:	Diarrhoea, itching.
Course:	Not appropriate.
Complications:	Severe dehydration, stress from irritation.
Treatment:	Anti-fungal drugs internally, vitamin B.
Outlook:	Fair.
Prevention:	Limit use of antibiotics and contraceptive pills. Vitamin B.

Gravity rating 2

Common name: **CATARACT**
Alternate name(s): Lens degeneration, lens opacity, white eye.
Cause: Congenital, injury, heat, radiation, diabetes, diet lack, drug effect, age deterioration.
Early symptoms: Vision poor in bad light.
Course: Double vision, opacity of lens.
Complications: Blindness on affected side(s).
Treatment: Surgery.
Outlook: Good.
Prevention: Avoid excessive exposure to heat or radiation near eyes.
Gravity rating 1: See also diabetes.

Common name: **CEREBRAL PALSY**
Alternate name(s): Spastic paralysis.
Cause: Hereditary, birth injury, German measles and other infections of pregnant women.
Early symptoms: Multiple and variable, poor muscle control, hearing and sight defects, mental retardation.
Course: Variable.
Complications: Personal injury due to uncontrolled movements, infections.
Treatment: Special training and education as early as possible.
Outlook: Fair.
Prevention: Anti-rubella vaccination of all women *before* pregnancy, careful control of labour.
Gravity rating 2

Common name:	**CHICKEN POX**
Alternate name(s):	Varicella.
Cause:	Viral infection.
Early symptoms:	Slight fever, malaise.
Course:	Red spots – becoming blisters on body in crops. itching.
Complications:	Scarring due to secondary infection, spreads as shingles to older people.
Treatment:	Rest, soothing lotions, painkillers.
Outlook:	Good.
Prevention:	Avoid contact with infected persons.
Gravity rating 0:	See also shingles.

Common name:	**CHILBLAINS**
Alternate name(s):	Pernio.
Cause:	Exposure to cold damp conditions.
Early symptoms:	Extremities cold and tingling, skin red and raw.
Course:	Swelling, skin is locally destroyed.
Complications:	Infection.
Treatment:	Vasodilator drugs, soothing creams, warmth.
Outlook:	Good.
Prevention:	Avoid local chilling.
Gravity rating 0:	See also Raynaud's disease.

Common name:	**CHOLERA**
Alternate name(s):	Asiatic cholera.
Cause:	Infection with cholera germ.
Early symptoms:	Abdominal and muscular cramps, diarrhoea, vomiting.
Course:	Very low temperature, scanty, dark urine, collapse.
Complications:	Irreversible fall of blood pressure, pneumonia, dehydration.
Treatment:	Restore fluids and salts, antibiotics, warmth.
Outlook:	Fair.
Prevention:	Vaccination, food hygiene, boil water, sanitation.
Gravity rating 3:	See also gastro-enteritis.

Common name:	**CHOREA**
Alternate name(s):	St Vitus' dance.
Cause:	Streptococcal infection.
Early symptoms:	Facial grimaces, twitching of muscles.
Course:	Not appropriate.
Complications:	Emotional instability.
Treatment:	Sedation.
Outlook:	Good.
Prevention:	Treatment of streptococcal infections.

Gravity rating 2

Common name:	**CIRRHOSIS OF LIVER**
Alternate name(s):	Hepatic cirrhosis, hob-nail liver, gin-drinker's liver.
Cause:	Excessive alcohol, infections, toxins.
Early symptoms:	Loss of appetite, distended abdomen, swollen ankles.
Course:	Vomiting blood, weight loss, jaundice.
Complications:	Severe haemorrhage, pancreatitis, anaemia.
Treatment:	High protein diet, vitamins, blood transfusion, transplant.
Outlook:	Poor.
Prevention:	Moderation in alcohol.
Gravity rating 4:	See also alcoholism, pancreatitis.

Common name:	**COELIAC DISEASE**
Alternate name(s):	Malabsorption syndrome, gluten intolerance, sprue.
Cause:	Congenital.
Early symptoms:	Foul diarrhoea after eating gluten containing foods.
Course:	Abdomen swollen, sore mouth.
Complications:	Stunted growth, malnutrition, anaemia, infection, neuritis.
Treatment:	Diet, iron, vitamins, folic acid.
Outlook:	Good.
Prevention:	Exclusion of gluten from diet.
Gravity rating 2	

Common name:	**COLD SORES**
Alternate name(s):	Herpes simplex.
Cause:	Infection with virus.
Early symptoms:	Tingling on lip occasionally elsewhere.
Course:	Blisters.
Complications:	Secondary bacterial infection, spread elsewhere.
Treatment:	Anti-viral cream.
Outlook:	Good.
Prevention:	Avoid small lip injuries, ultra-violet screening cream.

Gravity rating 1

Common name:	**COLIC**
Alternate name(s):	Abdominal cramps.
Cause:	Bowel obstruction, excessive gas formation, infection.
Early symptoms:	Recurrent painful cramps.
Course:	Vomiting.
Complications:	Total obstruction.
Treatment:	Anti-spasmodic drugs, treatment of cause, surgery.
Outlook:	Good depending on cause.
Prevention:	Dietary care.
Gravity rating 1:	See also appendicitis, gastro-enteritis, colitis, diverticulitis.

Common name:	**COLITIS**
Alternate name(s):	Large bowel inflammation.
Cause:	Multiple: infection, congenital, stress.
Early symptoms:	Diarrhoea, abdominal cramps.
Course:	Bloody bowel motions, severe collapse.
Complications:	Haemorrhage, obstruction, perforation of bowel.
Treatment:	Investigation, antibiotics, anti–spasmodics, diet.
Outlook:	Fair.
Prevention:	Avoid foods or situations known to cause attacks.
Gravity rating 2:	See also colic, diverticulitis, ulcerative colitis, Crohn's disease, irritable bowel syndrome.

Common name:	**CONGENITAL HEART DISEASE**
Alternate name(s):	Blue baby, Fallot's tetralogy, hole in the heart.
Cause:	German measles in mother, often unknown.
Early symptoms:	Cyanosis, breathlessness.
Course:	Failure to thrive.
Complications:	Generalised infections, rheumatic fever, cot death.
Treatment:	Surgery in selected cases.
Outlook:	Fair.
Prevention:	Avoid infections, toxic drugs and alcohol in pregnancy. Rubella vaccination before pregnancy.

Gravity rating 4

Common name:	**CONJUNCTIVITIS**
Alternate name(s):	Red eye, pink eye.
Cause:	Infection, excess glaring light, irritants.
Early symptoms:	Soreness in eye, excess tears.
Course:	Pus from eye, light hurts, lids stuck together.
Complications:	Becoming chronic.
Treatment:	Antibiotic eye drops, dark glasses.
Outlook:	Good.
Prevention:	Protective glasses at work, personal hygiene.
Gravity rating 1:	See also styes, trachoma, blepharitis.

Common name:	**CONSTIPATION. (SIMPLE)**
Alternate name(s):	Costiveness.
Cause:	Diet, bad habits, (e.g. neglecting the urge to pass bowel motions), prescribed medications, excess purgatives.
Early symptoms:	Difficulty having bowel motion.
Course:	Severe difficulty.
Complications:	Obstruction, piles.
Treatment:	Re-education of bowel, diet, mild laxatives, suppositories, exercise.
Outlook:	Good.
Prevention:	Maintain regularity.
Gravity rating 1:	

Common name:	**CORONARY THROMBOSIS**
Alternate name(s):	Acute coronary insufficiency, heart attack, coronary.
Cause:	Sudden obstruction of a heart artery by a clot.
Early symptoms:	Acute gripping chest pain, sweating, weakness.
Course:	Collapse.
Complications:	Fluid in lungs, sudden death, chronic disability.
Treatment:	Rest, pain relief, oxygen, anti-clotting drugs.
Outlook:	Fair.
Prevention:	Coronary by-pass surgery in some cases, stop smoking, reduce weight, adjust life style.
Gravity rating 4:	See also angina pectoris.

Common name:	**COT DEATH**
Alternate name(s):	Sudden infant death syndrome, SIDS.
Cause:	Congenital heart disease, allergy, infection, unknown.
Early symptoms:	Previously healthy baby found dead.
Course:	Not appropriate.
Complications:	Parents often suffer severe psychological stress and require bereavement counselling.
Treatment:	Not appropriate.
Outlook:	Not appropriate.
Prevention:	Frequent checks on babies, electronic monitoring.
Gravity rating 5	

Common name:	**CROHN'S DISEASE**
Alternate name(s):	Regional ileitis.
Cause:	Unknown.
Early symptoms:	Lower abdominal pain, flatulence.
Course:	Bloody diarrhoea, weight loss, anaemia.
Complications:	Peritonitis, perforation, fistula on to skin, anaemia, malnutrition.
Treatment:	Symptomatic, steroids, antibiotics, pain relief, surgery.
Outlook:	Poor.
Prevention:	None known.
Gravity rating 4:	See also colitis.

Common name:	**CROUP**
Alternate name(s):	Laryngeal spasm.
Cause:	Infection or foreign body in throat, allergy.
Early symptoms:	Noisy, wheezing breathing, barking cough.
Course:	Distressed breathing, face purple.
Complications:	Severe respiratory obstruction.
Treatment:	Treat cause, remove foreign body, steam inhalations, anti-allergy drugs, emergency surgery.
Outlook:	Good.
Prevention:	Adequate treatment of throat infections, keep small objects away from small children.
Gravity rating 3:	See also diphtheria, bronchitis, laryngitis, tonsillitis.

Common name:	**CYSTIC FIBROSIS**
Alternate name(s):	Mucoviscidosis.
Cause:	Hereditary metabolic defect.
Early symptoms:	Difficulty breathing, poor nutrition, cough, sweating.
Course:	Vomiting, abdominal swelling, diarrhoea, salt loss.
Complications:	Repeated infections, severe malnutrition.
Treatment:	Pancreatic extracts, drugs to loosen sputum, antibiotics, diet, postural drainage, heart lung transplant.
Outlook:	Poor.
Prevention:	Genetic counselling before conception.

Gravity rating 4

Common name:	**CYSTITIS**
Alternate name(s):	Chill on the bladder.
Cause:	Infection of urinary bladder.
Early symptoms:	Frequency of urination, stinging pain passing urine, shivering.
Course:	Blood in urine.
Complications:	Becomes chronic.
Treatment:	Fluids, rest, antibiotics, pain relief.
Outlook:	Good.
Prevention:	Avoid chilling, local hygiene, treat infections elsewhere.

Gravity rating 2

Common name:	**DEAFNESS** ***A) CONDUCTIVE DEAF-*** ***NESS***
Alternate name (s):	Conductive deafness.
Cause:	Obstruction within ear(s), wax, fluid, injury, infection.
Early symptoms:	Sudden or gradual onset of deafness.
Course:	May clear spontaneously.
Complications:	Chronic damage.
Treatment:	Remove cause.
Outlook:	Good.
Prevention:	Gently ear toilette, treat respiratory infections.
Gravity rating 1:	See also otitis, otalgia.

	B) NERVE DEAFNESS
Alternate name(s):	Not appropriate.
Cause:	Damage to nerve(s) of hearing by trauma, tumour, infection, congenital due to maternal infection.
Early symptoms:	Tinnitus, usually gradual onset of deafness.
Course:	Steady increase of deafness.
Complications:	Psychic stress.
Treatment:	Treat cause, lip reading.
Outlook:	Fair.
Prevention:	Early investigation of hearing problems, rubella vaccination of girls.
Gravity rating 2:	See also tinnitus, meningitis, German measles.

C) WILLIS'S DEAFNESS

Alternate name(s):	Boilermakers' deafness, disco deafness.
Cause:	Long term exposure to loud noise.
Early symptoms:	Rapid onset of hearing difficulty in a young person.
Course:	Total deafness.
Complications:	Psychological distress, employment problems.
Treatment:	None, hearing aid, learn lip reading.
Outlook:	Poor.
Prevention:	Avoid continuous loud noise, wear ear pads at work.

Gravity rating 2

Common name:	**DELIRIUM TREMENS**
Alternate name(s):	DTs, the horrors, the jigs.
Cause:	Alcoholic excess.
Early symptoms:	Nervousness, tension, depression.
Course:	Hallucinations, extreme terror.
Complications:	Pneumonia, injury.
Treatment:	Gradual withdrawal of alcohol, sedation, vitamin B.
Outlook:	Fair.
Prevention:	Avoid alcohol, gradual reduction in heavy drinker.
Gravity rating 3:	See also drug abuse, alcoholism.

Common name: **DENTAL CARIES**
Alternate name(s): Tooth decay.
Cause: Poor dental hygiene, deficient diet, excess sugar in diet.
Early symptoms: Small holes in teeth.
Course: Holes enlarge, pain, infection.
Complications: Root abscess, spread of infection.
Treatment: Repair, deal with infection, extraction.
Outlook: Good.
Prevention: Regular dental checks, mouth hygiene, dental sealant.

Gravity rating 1

Common name: **DEPRESSION**
Alternate name(s): Melancholia.
Cause: Excessive reaction to events, unknown.
Early symptoms: Excess fatigue, insomnia, agitation, withdrawal, irritability.
Course: Paranoia, suspicion, self-hate, apathy.
Complications: Suicide.
Treatment: Anti-depressive drugs, ECT, psychotherapy.
Outlook: Fair.
Prevention: None known.
Gravity rating 3: See also manic depression, schizophrenia.

Common name:	**DEVIL'S GRIP**
Alternate name(s):	Pleurodynia, Bornholm disease.
Cause:	Inflammation of pleura by virus.
Early symptoms:	Sharp pain in chest on breathing, headache, sore throat.
Course:	Not appropriate.
Complications:	Pneumonia.
Treatment:	Bed rest, pain killers.
Outlook:	Good.
Prevention:	None known.
Gravity rating 1:	See also pleurisy.

Common name:	**DIABETES**
Alternate name(s):	Excess blood sugar.
Cause:	Failure of pancreas to produce insulin.
Early symptoms:	Weight loss (or gain), thirst, frequency, itching.
Course:	Damage to eyes, nerves, kidneys, blood vessels.
Complications:	Coma, blindness, infections, gangrene.
Treatment:	Diet, insulin type drugs, skin hygiene, controlled exercise.
Outlook:	Fair.
Prevention:	Regular checks to detect early onset.
Gravity rating 3:	See also cataract, hypoglycaemia.

Common name: **DIPHTHERIA**
Alternate name(s): Not appropriate.
Cause: Infection with diphtheria germ.
Early symptoms: Sore throat, temperature.
Course: Obstruction to breathing, croup, swollen neck glands.
Complications: Heart failure, kidney damage.
Treatment: Anti-toxin, rest, antibiotics, surgery for choking.
Outlook: Fair.
Prevention: Vaccination, sanitation, personal hygiene.
Gravity rating 3: See also croup.

Common name: **DISLOCATION**
Alternate name(s): Displacement of a bone from its joint.
Cause: Sudden strain.
Early symptoms: Acute pain, inability to move joint.
Course: Not appropriate.
Complications: Fracture, later arthritis.
Treatment: Replacement, rest, physiotherapy, pain relief.
Outlook: Good.
Prevention: Avoid sudden strains.
Gravity rating 1: See also fractures.

Common name:	**DIVERTICULITIS**
Alternate name(s):	Not appropriate.
Cause:	Inflammation of small pockets in large intestine.
Early symptoms:	Abdominal cramps, mainly on left side.
Course:	Episodes of diarrhoea, with pus and blood sometimes.
Complications:	Rupture of pus filled pocket, peritonitis.
Treatment:	Diet, anti-spasmodics, antibiotics in acute flares, enemas, surgery.
Outlook:	Good.
Prevention:	None known.
Gravity rating 2:	See also colitis, Crohn's disease, ulcerative colitis.

Common name:	**DOWN'S SYNDROME.**
Alternate name(s):	Mongolism.
Cause:	Congenital, older parents.
Early symptoms:	Characteristic appearance.
Course:	Other defects may become apparent.
Complications:	Heart failure, infections, family stresses.
Treatment:	Social help, special education.
Outlook:	Poor.
Prevention:	Pre-conception counselling.
Gravity rating 4:	

DRUG ABUSE AND ADDICTION.

Drug addiction has been known for centuries particularly in the Far East. Within the last couple of decades it has become a major social problem throughout the world made ever more serious by the relationship between drug injection and AIDS.

The drug addict is the main sufferer but others are inevitably involved. As well as suffering mental distress a family may be financially drained by paying for deliberate crimes and accidental injuries following one member's addiction. Reckless driving under the influence of drugs may result in serious injuries and death for total strangers. Most tragic or all drug related events is the birth of a mentally or physically handicapped baby already dependent on the drugs taken by its mother during pregnancy.

Treatment of drug addiction is not easy and takes a long time. Because of severe emotional and physical withdrawal symptoms primary treatment is best carried out as an in-patient in a fully equipped centre. After detoxification and discharge follow-up treatment by the family doctor, an out-patient hospital department and other social services is vital. It is an unfortunate fact of life that most addicts are devious and will go to any lengths to get money to fuel their habit so that families must always be alert to avoid being conned. Firm, consistent, positive, non-judgemental support is the best help which families can give their drug dependent members. There are drug treatment centres in most cities where advice and help can be obtained by worried families.

Substance:	**ALCOHOL**
Alternate name(s):	Liquor, booze, hootch, moonshine.
Method of use:	By mouth.
Early symptoms:	Excessive social drinking, rapid drinking, secret drinking.
Late symptoms:	Morning after drinking, deterioration of work performance, blackouts, amnesia.
Complications:	Liver damage, social problems with work, driving, personal relations, brain damage, cancer, impotence, neuritis.
Treatment:	Depends on addict's motivation. Psychological help, vitamin B, aversion therapy, referral to Alcoholics Anonymous.
Withdrawal : symptoms	Insomnia, tremors, anxiety, tension, delirium tremens.

Substance:	**AMPHETAMINES**
Alternate name(s):	Pep pills, uppers, speed, jolly beans.
Method of use:	By mouth, later injection.
Early symptoms:	Excessive alertness, restless, insomnia, rapid speech.
Late symptoms:	Confusion, tremors, profuse sweating, headaches, pallor.
Complications:	Malnutrition, infection if injected, aggression, rise in blood pressure, AIDS and hepatitis from shared syringes.
Treatment:	Rapid controlled withdrawal, sedation.
Withdrawal: symptoms	Excess fatigue, depression.

Substance:	**BARBITURATES**
Alternate name(s):	Hypnotics, downers, goof-balls, yellow jackets.
Method of use:	By mouth, later injection.
Early symptoms:	Faulty judgement, amnesia, mild confusion, slurred speech.
Late symptoms:	Confusion, depression, poor co-ordination.
Complications:	Suicide, potentiation by alcohol, AIDS, hepatitis.
Treatment:	Gradual controlled withdrawal, psychotherapy.
Withdrawal: *symptoms*	Insomnia, tension, convulsions, low blood pressure, delirium,falling.

Substance:	**COCAINE**
Alternate name(s):	Coke, snow, flake, leaf.
Method of use:	Sniffing, injection.
Early symptoms:	Episodes of elation often after brief absence from associates.
Late symptoms:	Nasal inflammation, muscular twitching, gastric upsets, hallucinations, irregular pulse.
Complications:	Aggressive anti-social behaviour, AIDS, hepatitis.
Treatment:	Group therapy with rehabilitated addicts.
Withdrawal symptoms:	Depression.

Substance:	**HEROIN**
Alternate name(s):	Diacetylmorphine, smack, horse, junk, snort, speedball (with cocaine).
Method of use:	By mouth, inhalation, smoking, injection.
Early symptoms:	Drowsiness, mood changes, stupor, needle marks, small pupils.
Late symptoms:	Anti-social behaviour.
Complications:	Malnutrition, hepatitis, septicaemia, law-breaking, AIDS.
Treatment:	Hospitalisation, controlled withdrawal.
Withdrawal: *symptoms*	Vomiting, abdominal pain, muscle cramps, sweating, diarrhoea.

Substance:	**LSD**
Alternate name(s):	Lysergic acid diethylamide, acid, cubes, zen, 25.
Method of use:	By mouth.
Early symptoms:	Disorientation, unfounded fear, erratic behaviour, body odour.
Late symptoms:	Hallucinations, nightmares, depression.
Complications:	Accidental suicide from failure to appreciate danger.
Treatment:	Controlled withdrawal.
Withdrawal: *symptoms*	Not appropriate.

Substance:	**MARIJUANA**
Alternate name(s):	Cannabis, hash, hashish, tea, pot, grass, weed, hemp, Mary Jane.
Method of use:	Smoking.
Early symptoms:	Erratic behaviour, odour of burnt rope, plant found, red eyes.
Late symptoms:	Psychological dependence.
Complications:	Transition to hard drugs.
Treatment:	Withdrawal, psychotherapy.
Withdrawal : symptoms	Not appropriate.

Substance:	**MESCALINE**
Alternate name(s):	Mesc., cactus, button, peyote.
Method of use:	By mouth, injection.
Early symptoms:	Dilated pupils, rambling speech, nausea and diarrhoea.
Late symptoms:	Hallucinations, anxiety, panic reactions, coma.
Complications:	Prolonged hallucinations, brain damage, AIDS, hepatitis.
Treatment:	Rapid withdrawal, psychotherapy.
Withdrawal : symptoms	Anxiety.

Substance:	**OPIATES**
Alternate name(s):	Omnopon, morphine, codeine, diconal, dilaudid, DF 118, palfium, methadone, physeptone, temgesic.
Method of use:	By mouth, injection, smoking (in Far East).
Early symptoms:	Drowsiness, mood changes, pinpoint pupils.
Late symptoms:	Permanent sleepiness, anti-social behaviour.
Complications:	Malnutrition, hepatitis, septi-caemia, AIDS.
Treatment:	Hospitalisation for controlled withdrawal.
Withdrawal: symtpoms	Muscle spasm, vomiting, diarrhoea, sweating.

Substance:	**SOLVENTS**
Alternate name(s):	Glue, aerosols, petrol, lighter fluid, thinners, carbon tetrachloride, gas, propane, butane.
Method of use:	Inhalation.
Early symptoms:	Vertigo, mood swings, confusion, drunken appear-ance.
Late symptoms:	Weight loss, discovery of concealed solvents.
Complications:	Damage to vital organs, asphyxia, anaemia.
Treatment:	Firm non-judgemental guidance, supervision.
Withdrawal : symptoms	Not appropriate.

Common name:	**DYSMENORRHOEA**
Alternate name(s):	Periodic pain, monthly pain, menstrual pain.
Cause:	Often unknown, infection, fibroids.
Early symptoms:	Low abdominal and back pain.
Course:	Cramps, vomiting.
Complications:	Severe upset, interference with work and social life.
Treatment:	Anti-spasmodics, anti-inflammatory drugs, vitamin B6, surgery.
Outlook:	Fair.
Prevention:	Not appropriate.
Gravity rating 1:	See also fibroids.

Common name:	**DYSPAREUNIA**
Alternate name(s):	Painful intercourse.
Cause:	Local infection, inflexible vagina, anxiety, stress, aggressive partner.
Early symptoms:	Pain on intercourse.
Course:	Increasing pain and difficulty in sex leading sometimes to total failure.
Complications:	Psychological stress.
Treatment:	Remove local cause, gentle dilatation, lubricants, psychotherapy, relaxant drugs.
Outlook:	Fair.
Prevention:	Education and preparation of both partners for sexual intercourse.

Gravity rating 1

Common name:	**EARACHE**
Alternate name(s):	Otalgia, otitis.
Cause:	Ear infection usually from nasal passages.
Early symptoms:	Ear pain.
Course:	Purulent ear discharge.
Complications:	Spread to mastoid, deafness, chronic ear discharge.
Treatment:	Ear drops, antibiotics, painkillers.
Outlook:	Good.
Prevention:	Treat nose and throat infections.
Gravity rating 2:	See also deafness.

Common name:	**ECLAMPSIA**
Alternate name(s):	Pregnancy toxaemia.
Cause:	Unknown.
Early symptoms:	Blurred vision, headache, rise of blood pressure.
Course:	Swollen ankles, reduced urine output.
Complications:	Convulsions, coma.
Treatment:	Rest, sedation, salt-free diet, increase urine output.
Outlook:	Fair.
Prevention:	Regular pre-natal checks.
Gravity rating 3	

Common name: **ECTOPIC PREGNANCY**
Alternate name(s): Extra-uterine pregnancy, tubal pregnancy.
Cause: Embryo developing outside of womb.
Early symptoms: Lower abdominal pain.
Course: Collapse.
Complications: Severe haemorrhage.
Treatment: Surgery, blood transfusion.
Outlook: Good.
Prevention: None known, early ultra-sonic scan.

Gravity rating 3

Common name: **ECZEMA**
Alternate name(s): Dermatitis.
Cause: Allergic reaction.
Early symptoms: Skin red and itchy.
Course: Skin broken, blistering and scabbing.
Complications: Infection.
Treatment: Find and remove irritant, steroid creams.
Outlook: Fair.
Prevention: Avoid known allergens.
Gravity rating 2: See also allergy.

Common name:	**EMBOLISM**
Alternate name(s):	Not appropriate.
Cause:	Obstruction of a blood vessel by clots, fat, air, dead cells, tumour, foreign body.
Early symptoms:	Symptoms, treatment and outlook depend on size and site of the blockage.
Course:	Not appropriate.
Complications:	Blockage of vital organ's artery.
Treatment:	Anti-coagulant drugs, surgery.
Outlook:	Fair.
Prevention:	Active movement after surgery, support of vein injuries.
Gravity rating 4:	See also thrombosis, varicose veins, endocarditis.

Common name:	**EMPHYSEMA**
Alternate name(s):	COAD – chronic obstructive airways disease.
Cause:	Long term damage to small air cells in lungs.
Early symptoms:	Breathlessness.
Course:	Cyanosis of skin, barrel shape of chest, very breathless.
Complications:	Chronic infection, asthma, heart failure.
Treatment:	Stop smoking, oxygen, bronchodilator drugs, physiotherapy.
Outlook:	Poor.
Prevention:	Avoid dusty work, wear dust mask, treat infections, no smoking.
Gravity rating 4:	See also bronchitis, bronchiectasis, asthma.

Common name:	**EMPYEMA**
Alternate name(s):	Pus in body cavity usually chest.
Cause:	Lung infection.
Early symptoms:	Pleurisy.
Course:	Temperature, breathlessness.
Complications:	Septicaemia.
Treatment:	Antibiotics, surgery.
Outlook:	Good.
Prevention:	Adequate treatment of chest infections.
Gravity rating 3:	See also pneumonia, pleurisy.

Common name:	**ENCEPHALITIS**
Alternate name(s):	Brain fever.
Cause:	Viral or bacterial infection of brain.
Early symptoms:	Headache, temperature, nausea.
Course:	Confusion, paralysis, coma.
Complications:	Permanent brain damage.
Treatment:	Antibiotics, supportive treatment, rehabilitation.
Outlook:	Fair.
Prevention:	Not appropriate.
Gravity rating 4:	See also meningitis.

Common name:	**ENDOCARDITIS**
Alternate name(s):	Valvular heart disease.
Cause:	Infection of internal lining of heart, rheumatic fever.
Early symptoms:	Irregular temperature, shivering, multiple pains.
Course:	Anaemia, severe general disturbance.
Complications:	Emboli, heart and kidney failure.
Treatment:	Anitbiotics, bed rest, sedation, blood transfusion, heart valve replacement.
Outlook:	Fair.
Prevention:	Antibiotics before minor surgery in rheumatic or cardiac patients.
Gravity rating 4:	See also septicaemia, embolism, heart failure.

Common name:	**ENDOMETRITIS**
Alternate name(s):	Inflammation of the lining of the womb.
Cause:	Unknown, occasionally infection or tumour.
Early symptoms:	Temperature, lower abdominal pain.
Course:	Haemorrhage, purulent discharge.
Complications:	May become chronic.
Treatment:	Antibiotics, curetting, hysterectomy in some cases.
Outlook:	Good.
Prevention:	None known.
Gravity rating 2:	See also metrorrhagia.

Common name:	**ENURESIS**
Alternate name(s):	Bed wetting.
Cause:	Poor bladder control at night with many causes.
Early symptoms:	Urine passed without waking.
Course:	Not appropriate.
Complications:	Infection of skin, psychological stress.
Treatment:	Find cause, control infections, psychotherapy, no scolding, wet-bed alarm.
Outlook:	Variable.
Prevention:	Reduce fluid intake in evening, regular potting, training.
Gravity rating 1:	See also cystitis.

Common name:	**EPIDIDIMYTIS**
Alternate name(s):	Testicular duct infection.
Cause:	Mumps, venereal disease.
Early symptoms:	Soreness and swelling of scrotum.
Course:	Temperature, malaise.
Complications:	Sterility.
Treatment:	Bed rest, relief of pain, antibiotics.
Outlook:	Good.
Prevention:	Avoid infected sexual partners.
Gravity rating 2:	See also mumps, orchitis.

Common name:	**EPILEPSY (MAJOR)**
Alternate name(s):	The falling sickness, grand mal.
Cause:	Often unknown, may be injury or tumour.
Early symptoms:	Sudden convulsions of whole or part of body.
Course:	Loss of consciousness, temporary loss of bowel and bladder control.
Complications:	Injury by falling, hitting hard or hot objects.
Treatment:	Anti-epileptic drugs, occasionally surgery.
Outlook:	Good.
Prevention:	Regular administration of drugs, avoid known triggers, e.g. flashing lights.

Gravity rating 3

Common name:	**EPILEPSY (MINOR)**
Alternate name(s):	Petit mal, absences.
Cause:	Unknown.
Early symptoms:	Transient periods of vagueness.
Course:	Very slight twitching of muscles.
Complications:	Major epilepsy may develop later.
Treatment:	Specific drugs.
Outlook:	Good.
Prevention:	Regular medication.

Gravity rating 1

Common name:	**ERYSIPELAS**
Alternate name(s):	Cellulitis.
Cause:	Skin infection.
Early symptoms:	Skin red, painful, temperature.
Course:	Spread to deeper layers.
Complications:	Septicaemia.
Treatment:	Antibiotics.
Outlook:	Good.
Prevention:	Hygiene, clean small wounds.
Gravity rating 2:	See also septicaemia.

Common name:	**FAINTING**
Alternate name(s):	Syncope, blackout.
Cause:	Reduced circulation to brain, stress, fear, emotion.
Early symptoms:	Feeling of faintness.
Course:	Collapse.
Complications:	Injury in fall.
Treatment:	Lie flat with head lower than feet, rest.
Outlook:	Good.
Prevention:	Full examination to find cause.
Gravity rating 0:	See also hypotension, low blood pressure.

Common name:	**FIBROIDS**
Alternate name(s):	Benign womb tumours, fibromyomata.
Cause:	Unknown, less common in women who have had children.
Early symptoms:	Heavy menstrual bleeding, lower abdominal pain.
Course:	Bleeding between periods.
Complications:	Anaemia, malignant changes, infertility.
Treatment:	Surgery.
Outlook:	Good.
Prevention:	None known.
Gravity rating 2:	See also metrorrhagia, menorrhagia.

Common name:	**FIBROSITIS**
Alternate name(s):	Muscular rheumatism, fibromyalgic syndrome.
Cause:	Strain, local chilling, over exertion.
Early symptoms:	Pain and stiffness.
Course:	Small nodules form in muscles.
Complications:	May be symptom of another rheumatic condition.
Treatment:	Heat, rest, analgesics, steroids, physiotherapy.
Outlook:	Good.
Prevention:	Avoid strains and chilling.
Gravity rating 2:	See also arthritis, bursitis, rheumatism.

Common name:	**FOOD POISONING**
Alternate name(s):	Not appropriate.
Cause:	Eating infected food.
Early symptoms:	Nausea, cramps, vomiting, headache.
Course:	Severe diarrhoea.
Complications:	Dehydration in very young or old.
Treatment:	Replace fluid and salt loss, anti-spasmodics, antibiotics.
Outlook:	Good.
Prevention:	Scrupulous food hygiene.
Gravity rating 2:	See also gastro-enteritis.

Common name:	**FRACTURE**
Alternate name(s):	Broken bone.
Cause:	Direct or indirect violence, either accidental or deliberate.
Early symptoms:	Sudden, severe pain in area, limited or no use of limb.
Course:	Not appropriate.
Complications:	Infection or haemorrhage if skin is broken, distortion.
Treatment:	Rest, transport only if supported.
Outlook:	Good.
Prevention:	Avoid injuries.
Gravity rating 1	

Common name:	**GALL-BLADDER DISEASE**
	A) INFLAMMATION
Alternate name(s):	Cholecystitis.
Cause:	Obstruction of drainage from gall-bladder by infection, pressure or kinking.
Early symptoms:	Flatulence, discomfort in abdomen, heartburn.
Course:	Jaundice, vomiting, pale bowel motions, dark urine.
Complications:	Permanent obstruction.
Treatment:	Pain relief, non-fat diet, antibiotics, fluids, surgery.
Outlook:	Good.
Prevention:	Low-fat diet, exercise, avoid constipation, avoid alcohol.
Gravity rating 2:	See also liver, hepatitis, gallstones.

	B) GALLSTONES
Alternate name(s):	Biliary calculi, cholelithiasis.
Cause:	Long-term dietary faults and lack of exercise.
Early symptoms:	Upper abdominal discomfort after fatty meals, flatulence.
Course:	Severe bouts of pain, often referred to right shoulder.
Complications:	Obstruction of bile ducts, perforation of gall-bladder.
Treatment:	Surgery, stone-dissolving drugs, ultra-sound, antispasmodics.
Outlook:	Good.
Prevention:	Low-fat diet, stone-dissolving drugs.
Gravity rating 2	

Common name:	**GANGRENE**
Alternate name(s):	Tissue death.
Cause:	Local circulation failure, severe injuries.
Early symptoms:	Skin dark red and tender.
Course:	Skin black and necrotic or moist and purulent.
Complications:	Loss of limb, septicaemia.
Treatment:	Restoration of circulation, amputation.
Outlook:	Poor.
Prevention:	Maintenance of circulation.
Gravity rating 4:	See also arterio-sclerosis, bedsores, Raynaud's disease, scleroderma, Buerger's disease.

Common name:	**GASTRITIS**
Alternate name(s):	Inflamed stomach.
Cause:	Indigestible or excessive amounts of food, alcohol, infection, irritants.
Early symptoms:	Abdominal pain, nausea, headache.
Course:	Vomiting, temperature.
Complications:	Vomiting blood, collapse.
Treatment:	Rest, antacids, fluids, non-irritant painkillers.
Outlook:	Good.
Prevention:	Avoid known causes.
Gravity rating 1:	See also gastro-enteritis, peptic ulcer.

Common name:	**GASTRO-ENTERITIS**
Alternate name(s):	Gippy tummy, D&V, Delhi belly, Montezuma's revenge.
Cause:	Contaminated food.
Early symptoms:	Abdominal pain, vomiting, diarrhoea.
Course:	Not appropriate.
Complications:	Dehydration, collapse.
Treatment:	Rest, fluids, mineral salts, antibiotics, antacids.
Outlook:	Good.
Prevention:	Strict food hygiene.
Gravity rating 2:	See also gastritis, cholera, food poisoning.

Common name:	**GERMAN MEASLES**
Alternate name(s):	Rubella.
Cause:	Viral infection.
Early symptoms:	Vague malaise, small joint pains.
Course:	Diffuse rash, small glands in neck.
Complications:	Maternal infection may cause birth defects.
Treatment:	Bed rest and aspirin.
Outlook:	Good.
Prevention:	Vaccination of all girls. Pregnant women avoid contact with carriers.
Gravity rating 0	

Common name:	**GLANDULAR FEVER**
Alternate name(s):	Infectious mononucleosis, the kissing disease.
Cause:	Viral infection.
Early symptoms:	Sore throat, temperature.
Course:	Enlarged glands, painful joints.
Complications:	Jaundice, rupture of spleen, chronic invalidism, anaemia.
Treatment:	Bed rest, pain relief, steroids.
Outlook:	Good.
Prevention:	Avoid close contact with known cases.
Gravity rating 2	

Common name:	**GLAUCOMA**
Alternate name(s):	Raised eye pressure.
Cause:	Hereditary in some cases, myopia, diabetes.
Early symptoms:	Blurred vision, haloes around bright light.
Course:	Loss of side vision.
Complications:	Blindness.
Treatment:	Eye drops, tablets, surgery.
Outlook:	Fair.
Prevention:	Regular checks of eye pressure.
Gravity rating 3:	See also iritis.

Common name:	**GOITRE**
	A) SIMPLE GOITRE
Alternate name(s):	Hypothyroidism, thyroid deficiency, Hashimoto's disease.
Cause:	Iodine lack.
Early symptoms:	Slow enlargement of thyroid gland in neck.
Course:	Skin dry, general sluggishness, voice changes.
Complications:	Pressure on throat and blood vessels.
Treatment:	Thyroid tablets, surgery.
Outlook:	Good.
Prevention:	Iodine in drinking water.
Gravity rating 1	

	B) TOXIC GOITRE
Alternate name(s):	Grave's disease, exophthalmic goitre, hyperthyroidism.
Cause:	Overactive thyroid gland.
Early symptoms:	Rapid pulse, loss of weight, sweating, nervousness.
Course:	Bulging eyes, hand tremors, diarrhoea.
Complications:	Heart failure.
Treatment:	Drugs to reduce gland activity, surgery.
Outlook:	Fair.
Prevention:	None Known.
Gravity rating 2	

Common name:	**GONORRHOEA**
Alternate name(s):	The clap.
Cause:	Microbe transmitted sexually.
Early symptoms:	Stinging on passing water, increasing frequency of urinating.
Course:	Discharge of pus from genitals.
Complications:	Eye infection, arthritis, sterility, urinary obstruction.
Treatment:	Antibiotics, surgery for later obstruction.
Outlook:	Good.
Prevention:	Avoid infected sexual partner, condom, hygiene.
Gravity rating 2:	See also syphilis, AIDS, herpes.

Common name:	**GOUT (ACUTE)**
Alternate name(s):	Podagra, hyperuricaemia.
Cause:	Raised blood uric acid, hereditary, chemotherapy.
Early symptoms:	Increasing frequency of urinating, nausea, muscle and joint soreness.
Course:	Severe small joint pain and swelling.
Complications:	See chronic gout.
Treatment:	Pain relief, fluids, rest, padding sore joints.
Outlook:	Good.
Prevention:	Avoid minor injuries, control alcohol and red meat intake, regular drugs to reduce uric acid.
Gravity rating 2:	See also arthritis.

Common name:	**GOUT (CHRONIC)**
Alternate name(s):	Tophaceous gout.
Cause:	Raised uric acid, hereditary.
Early symptoms:	Pain in muscles and small joints.
Course:	Kidney colic, hard lumps in skin and cartilage.
Complications:	Heart involvement.
Treatment:	Drugs to reduce uric acid, high fluid intake, diet.
Outlook:	Fair.
Prevention:	Avoid excess alcohol, red meats and offal meats, use uric acid reducing drugs.

Gravity rating 2

Common name:	**HAEMATEMESIS**
Alternate name(s):	Vomiting blood.
Cause:	Symptom of several diseases.
Early symptoms:	Trace of blood on vomiting, black motions.
Course:	More severe bleeding.
Complications:	Collapse.
Treatment:	Full investigation, sedation, blood transfusion, surgery.
Outlook:	Depends on cause.
Prevention:	Early treatment of intestinal symptoms.
Gravity rating 3:	See also peptic ulcer, cancer, gastro-enteritis, cirrhosis of liver.

Common name:	**HAEMOPHILIA**
Alternate name(s):	Bleeder's disease, the Royal disease.
Cause:	Defective blood clotting, hereditary.
Early symptoms:	Minor cuts continue to bleed, severe bruising.
Course:	Internal and joint haemorrhages.
Complications:	Severe anaemia, AIDS from contaminated donor blood.
Treatment:	Blood transfusion, clotting concentrates.
Outlook:	Poor
Prevention:	Genetic counselling before conception, avoid contact sports, carry medicalert card.

Gravity rating 4

Common name:	**HAEMORRHOIDS**
Alternate name(s):	Piles, anal varicosities.
Cause:	Constipation, obstruction, hereditary, excessive purgation.
Early symptoms:	Blood on motions, itching, excess mucus.
Course:	Piles enlarge.
Complications:	Haemorrhage, clotting.
Treatment:	Suppositories, injection, surgery, pain relief.
Outlook:	Good.
Prevention:	Avoid constipation, strong purgation, inactivity.

Gravity rating 2

Common name:	**HAY FEVER**
Alternate name(s):	Allergic rhinitis, seasonal rhinitis.
Cause:	Allergy to pollen, dust, other irritants.
Early symptoms:	Running nose, sneezing, eye irritation, headache.
Course:	Recurs with exposure to specific irritant.
Complications:	Secondary infection, sinusitis, asthma.
Treatment:	Anti-histamine drugs, steroids, desensitisation, nasal spray.
Outlook:	Fair.
Prevention:	Avoid known allergens such as pollens etc., desensitisation.
Gravity rating 2:	See also allergy, asthma.

Common name:	**HEADACHE**
Alternate name(s):	Cephalgia.
Cause:	Symptom of many conditions trivial and serious.
Early symptoms:	Transient pain in head.
Course:	Becoming more severe and frequent.
Complications:	Related to underlying cause.
Treatment:	If simple measures do not relieve, medical investigation.
Outlook:	Depends on cause.
Prevention:	Avoid known triggers.
Gravity rating :	See also meningitis, migraine, blood pressure, sinusitis.

Common name:	**HEART BLOCK**
Alternate name(s):	Bradycardia, slow pulse.
Cause:	Interference with electrical impulse in heart due to arterio-sclerosis, infarct.
Early symptoms:	Very slow pulse, (below 50 per minute.)
Course:	Blackouts.
Complications:	Not appropriate.
Treatment:	Pacemaker.
Outlook:	Fair.
Prevention:	Not appropriate.
Gravity rating 3:	See also coronary, endocarditis, heart failure.

Common name:	**HEART FAILURE**
Alternate name(s):	Congestive cardiac failure, pump failure.
Cause:	Previous heart attack, endocarditis, blood pressure, congenital.
Early symptoms:	Swollen ankles, irregular pulse, breathlessness on slight exertion, blue lips, tiredness.
Course:	Increase of all symptoms, chest pain, swollen abdomen.
Complications:	Kidney failure, congestive pneumonia.
Treatment:	Increase fluid output, graduated activity, low–salt diet, pacemaker.
Outlook:	Fair.
Prevention:	Adequate treatment of initial heart problems.
Gravity rating 3:	See also angina, coronary disease, endocarditis, blood pressure, myocarditis, pericarditis.

Common name:	**HEATSTROKE**
Alternate name(s):	Sunstroke.
Cause:	Excess exposure to heat.
Early symptoms:	Faintness, nausea, headache, dizziness.
Course:	Temperature rises, cramp, rapid pulse, collapse.
Complications:	Heart and kidney failure.
Treatment:	Cold packs, replace salt and fluids.
Outlook:	Fair.
Prevention:	Avoid prolonged exposure to heat and sun.

Gravity rating 4

Common name:	**HEPATITIS**
	A) INFECTIOUS
	B) SERUM
Alternate name(s):	Liver infection.
Cause:	A. Viral infection spread by personal contact, food or water.
	B. Infection spread by contaminated syringes.
Early symptoms:	Nausea, loss of appetite, slight temperature.
Course:	Jaundice, vomiting, abdominal pain, dark urine, pale motions.
Complications:	Liver destruction, coma, depression.
Treatment:	Bed rest, steroids, antibiotics, diet, relief of symptoms.
Outlook:	Fair.
Prevention:	A. Food preparation hygiene, personal hygiene.
	B. No communal syringes, vaccination.
Gravity rating 4:	See also jaundice, liver, gallbladder, leptospirosis.

Common name: **HERNIA**
Alternate name(s): Rupture.
Cause: Coughing or straining forces bowel through weak area in wall of abdomen.
Early symptoms: Bulge in groin, navel, operation scar, elsewhere.
Course: Pain, increase in size.
Complications: Obstruction, bowel gangrene.
Treatment: Truss, surgery.
Outlook: Good.
Prevention: Avoid severe or prolonged straining, coughing, lifting.

Gravity rating 2

Common name: **HERPES (GENITAL)**
Alternate name(s): Not appropriate.
Cause: Virus infection of genital area.
Early symptoms: Blisters on sex organs.
Course: Blisters break down and become inflamed.
Complications: Secondary infection, generalised spread, later cancer.
Treatment: Anti-viral drugs locally and internally.
Outlook: Fair.
Prevention: Avoid infected sexual partners, use of condoms, good personal hygiene.
Gravity rating 2: See also gonorrhoea, syphilis, AIDS.

Common name:	**HIATUS HERNIA**
Alternate name(s):	Diaphragmatic hernia.
Cause:	Part of stomach or oesophagus bulges through flabby opening in diaphragm.
Early symptoms:	Indigestion, heartburn, flatulence, regurgitation.
Course:	Pain, difficulty swallowing.
Complications:	Haemorrhage, ulceration.
Treatment:	Antacids for acute symptoms, surgery.
Outlook:	Fair.
Prevention:	Avoid heavy spicy foods, lose weight, elevate head of bed.
Gravity rating 2:	See also gastritis, oesophagitis.

Common name:	**HIVES**
Alternate name(s):	Urticaria, nettle rash.
Cause:	Allergic reaction.
Early symptoms:	Red or white weals on body.
Course:	Become widespread with severe itching.
Complications:	Spread to airways with obstruction to breathing.
Treatment:	Anti-histamine medicines by mouth or injection,steroids, anti-itching creams.
Outlook:	Good unless airways are involved.
Prevention:	Avoid known allergens.
Gravity rating 2:	See also allergy, eczema.

Common name:	**HODGKIN'S DISEASE**
Alternate name(s):	Lymphadenoma.
Cause:	Unknown.
Early symptoms:	Painless enlargement of lymph glands, spleen, liver.
Course:	Progressive enlargement, fatigue, temperature.
Complications:	Pressure on vital organs, anaemia.
Treatment:	Radiation, cytotoxic drugs, transfusion, surgery, steroids.
Outlook:	Fair.
Prevention:	None known.
Gravity rating 4:	See also leukaemia, cancer.

Common name:	**HYDROCEPHALUS**
Alternate name(s):	Water on the brain.
Cause:	Normal drainage of fluid from the brain obstructed.
Early symptoms:	Infant's skull enlarged at or shortly after birth.
Course:	Convulsions.
Complications:	Mental retardation, associated spina bifida, other defects.
Treatment:	Surgery.
Outlook:	Fair.
Prevention:	None known.
Gravity rating 4:	See also spina bifida.

Common name:	**HYPERACTIVITY**
Alternate name(s):	Abnormal activity in a child.
Cause:	Possibly allergic reaction to certain foods.
Early symptoms:	Child over-active, restless, insomniac.
Course:	Cannot settle to study.
Complications:	Aggression, violence, anti-social behaviour.
Treatment:	Search for possible cause, eliminate foods in turn, parental counselling.
Outlook:	Fair.
Prevention:	Not appropriate.
Gravity rating 2	

Common name:	**HYPERPARATHYROIDISM**
Alternate name(s):	Over-active parathyroid glands.
Cause:	Tumour of parathyroid gland(s).
Early symptoms:	Thirst, increasing frequency of urination, back and joint pains, nausea.
Course:	Vomiting, bones become brittle, fractures.
Complications:	Kidney stones, bone deformities.
Treatment:	Surgery.
Outlook:	Good.
Prevention:	None.
Gravity rating 2:	See also rickets, osteomalacia.

Common name: **HYPOGLYCAEMIA**
Alternate name(s): Low blood sugar.
Cause: Starvation, pancreatic
tumour, excess anti–diabetic
drugs.
Early symptoms: Sweating, giddiness, hunger.
Course: Confusion, blackout.
Complications: Brain damage.
Treatment: Glucose by mouth or
injection, surgery for tumour.
Outlook: Fair.
Prevention: Regular food intake, proper
dosage of drugs for diabetes.
Gravity rating 3:   See also diabetes.

Common name: **HYPOTHERMIA**
Alternate name(s): Very low body temperature.
Cause: Exposure to cold.
Early symptoms: Lethargy, confusion.
Course: Deep coma.
Complications: Pneumonia, brain damage.
Treatment: Gradual warming, oxygen,
fluids, antibiotics.
Outlook: Good.
Prevention: Avoid chilling, supervision of
people at risk.

Gravity rating 3

Common name:	**IMPETIGO**
Alternate name(s):	Tetter, scrumpox.
Cause:	Bacterial infection of skin.
Early symptoms:	Patch of reddening, small blisters.
Course:	Pus forms, infection spread by scratching.
Complications:	Generalised infection, spread to kidneys.
Treatment:	Local antiseptic or antibiotic preparations.
Outlook:	Good.
Prevention:	Good personal hygiene.
Gravity rating 1:	See also boils, eczema, barber's rash.

Common name:	**INCONTINENCE (URINARY)**
Alternate name(s):	Leaking bladder.
Cause:	Multiple, including injury, infection, brain or spinal cord damage.
Early symptoms:	Brief episodes of loss of control.
Course:	Continuous dribbling.
Complications:	Local and widespread infection.
Treatment:	Underlying cause, local cleansing, catheter.
Outlook:	Poor.
Prevention:	Treatment of cause.
Gravity rating 3	

Common name:	**INFERTILITY (FEMALE)**
Alternate name(s):	Sterility.
Cause:	Obstruction of Fallopian tubes, chronic infection, immature womb, stress, gland deficiency.
Early symptoms:	Inability to conceive.
Course:	Not appropriate.
Complications:	Psychological stress, friction with partner.
Treatment:	Full investigation of both partners, surgery, artificial insemination by husband or donor (AID or AIH).
Outlook:	Fair.
Prevention:	Avoid sexual infection, full treatment of abdominal infection in youth.
Gravity rating 1:	See also male infertility.

Common name:	**INFERTILITY (MALE)**
Alternate name(s):	Inability to father a child.
Cause:	Impotence, injury, lack of sperm, chronic infection, mumps.
Early symptoms:	Failure to impregnate partner.
Course:	Not appropriate.
Complications:	Psychological stress, depression, friction.
Treatment:	Full investigation of both partners, AIH, AID.
Outlook:	Fair.
Prevention:	Avoid risk of venereal infections, mumps vaccination.
Gravity rating 1:	See also female infertility, orchitis.

Common name:	**INFLUENZA**
Alternate name(s):	Flu, *la grippe*.
Cause:	Viral infection.
Early symptoms:	Slight temperature, shivering, muscle pains, cough.
Course:	Chest pains, sweating, headache.
Complications:	Pneumonia, ME (myalgic encephalomyelitis), myocarditis.
Treatment:	Bed rest, painkillers, fluids.
Outlook:	Good.
Prevention:	Good nutrition, vaccination, avoid contact with others.
Gravity rating 1:	See also pneumonia, myalgic encephalomyelitis, myocarditis.

Common name:	**INSOMNIA**
Alternate name(s):	Sleeplessness.
Cause:	Multiple, such as noise, excess heat or cold, discomfort, pain, worry, depression, full stomach or bladder.
Early symptoms:	Broken sleep.
Course:	Severe sleep disturbance.
Complications:	Excess fatigue, psychosis.
Treatment:	Treat cause, relaxation therapy.
Outlook:	Variable.
Prevention:	Avoid cause.
Gravity rating 1	

Common name:	**IRITIS**
Alternate name(s):	Inflammation of iris of eye.
Cause:	Infection, injury, complication of other diseases.
Early symptoms:	Eye red and painful, headache, excessive tears.
Course:	Eye swollen and discoloured, pupil small, light hurts.
Complications:	Glaucoma, chronically impaired vision.
Treatment:	Treat cause, atropine drops, local antibiotics, pain relief, tinted glasses.
Outlook:	Fair.
Prevention:	Treatment of possible causes.
Gravity rating 3:	See also conjunctivitis, glaucoma.

Common name:	**IRRITABLE BOWEL SYNDROME**
Alternate name(s):	IBS, spastic colon, mucous colitis.
Cause:	Uncertain, stress.
Early symptoms:	Slimy diarrhoea, constipation, abdominal cramps, flatulence.
Course:	Back pain, distention, fatigue.
Complications:	Bleeding, psychological stress.
Treatment:	Full examiantion, diet, sedatives, anti-spasmodics.
Outlook:	Fair.
Prevention:	None known.
Gravity rating 2:	See also colitis, diarrhoea.

Common name:	**KERATOSIS**
Alternate name(s):	Horny skin, corn, callus.
Cause:	Chronic irritation, excessive sunlight.
Early symptoms:	Skin roughened and sore.
Course:	Skin thickened, painful on pressure, bleeding.
Complications:	Infection, malignant change.
Treatment:	Remove cause, surgery.
Outlook:	Good.
Prevention:	Avoid irritation and pressure.
Gravity rating 1:	See also cancer.

Common name:	**KETOSIS**
Alternate name(s):	Acid blood, ketoacidosis.
Cause:	Neglected diabetes.
Early symptoms:	Excess thirst, panting, smell of acetone on breath.
Course:	Not appropriate.
Complications:	Coma.
Treatment:	Fluids, insulin, dietary and insulin review.
Outlook:	Fair.
Prevention:	Strict adherence to diabetic regime.
Gravity rating 4:	See also diabetes, hypoglycaemia.

Common name:	**KYPHOSIS**
Alternate name(s):	Spinal curvature, hunchback.
Cause:	Injury, infection, senile deterioration.
Early symptoms:	Aching back pain.
Course:	Marked increase of normal or abnormal spinal curves.
Complications:	Pressure on spinal cord or nerves, paralysis.
Treatment:	Physiotherapy, surgery, brace.
Outlook:	Fair.
Prevention:	Avoid improper posture, treat injury or infection.
Gravity rating 2:	See also paraplegia, sciatica, osteoporosis.

Common name:	**LARYNGITIS.**
Alternate name(s):	Not appropriate.
Cause:	Inflammation of the voice box, viral, allergic, irritant.
Early symptoms:	Hoarseness, dry cough, temperature.
Course:	Loss of voice.
Complications:	Spread of infection.
Treatment:	Soothing syrups, inhalations, antibiotics.
Outlook:	Good.
Prevention:	Avoid irritants, stop smoking.
Gravity rating 1:	See also tonsillitis, sore throat.

Common name:	**LEPROSY**
	A) Nodular
	B) Neural
Alternate name(s):	Hansen's disease.
Cause:	Infection with leprosy bacillus.
Early symptoms:	Skin patches becoming hard and painful.
Course:	A. Gross facial distortion, scarring of tongue, mouth. B. Loss of pain sense, muscle wasting, gangrene.
Complications:	Cataracts, glaucoma, heart and sex gland involvement.
Treatment:	Special antibiotics, physiotherapy, psychological advice.
Outlook:	Fair.
Prevention:	Good personal hygiene if in contact with patient.
Gravity rating 3	

Common name:	**LEPTOSPIROSIS**
Alternate name(s):	Weil's disease, infectious jaundice.
Cause:	Infection from water or food contaminated by animals.
Early symptoms:	Temperature, shivering, nausea, vomiting.
Course:	Rashes, skin and mucous membrane bleeding, jaundice.
Complications:	Permanent kidney and liver damage.
Treatment:	Antibiotics, fluids, transfusion.
Outlook:	Fair.
Prevention:	Hygiene, protection of open cuts when handling animals.
Gravity rating 2:	See also hepatitis.

Common name:	**LEUKAEMIA**
Alternate name(s):	Blood cancer.
Cause:	Hereditary, excess radiation, toxic chemicals.
Early symptoms:	Undue fatigue, pallor, swollen glands, nose bleeds, sore throat.
Course:	Swollen internal organs, sweating, weight loss.
Complications:	Haemorrhage, involvement of vital organs.
Treatment:	Radiation, cytotoxic drugs, transfusion, bone marrow transplant, steroids.
Outlook:	Fair.
Prevention:	Avoid possible known causes.
Gravity rating 4:	See also cancer, Hodgkin's disease.

Common name:	**LEUKOPLAKIA**
Alternate name(s):	Chronic mouth irritation.
Cause:	Dentures, over-spiced food, excess tobacco.
Early symptoms:	Thick white patches in mouth.
Course:	Pain on talking or swallowing.
Complications:	Infection, malignant change.
Treatment:	Remove cause, mouth hygiene, curetting.
Outlook:	Good.
Prevention:	Good mouth hygiene, good dentures, avoid irritants.
Gravity rating 1	

Common name:	**LUMBAGO**
Alternate name(s):	Low back pain.
Cause:	Strain, injury, disc compression, degeneration, tumour.
Early symptoms:	Slight to severe pain in lower back, stiffness.
Course:	Pain radiates to leg(s), locked position.
Complications:	Permanent injury to sciatic nerve(s).
Treatment:	Rest, pain relief, anti-spasmodics, heat, physiotherapy, splinting, surgery.
Outlook:	Good.
Prevention:	Proper posture and lifting.
Gravity rating 3:	See also osteoarthritis, osteoporosis, osteomalacia, slipped disc.

Common name:	**LUNG ABSCESS**
Alternate name(s):	Localised lung infection.
Cause:	Pneumonia, obstruction from inhaled object or tumour.
Early symptoms:	Dry cough, chest pain, breathlessness.
Course:	Temperature, shivering, foul sputum.
Complications:	Permanent lung damage, secondary abscess in brain, haemorrhage.
Treatment:	Antibiotics, postural drainage, surgery.
Outlook:	Fair.
Prevention:	Early removal of obstruction by aspiration or surgery.
Gravity rating 3:	See also pneumonia, bronchiectasis.

Common name:	**LUPUS ERYTHEMATOSIS**
Alternate name(s):	LE.
Cause:	Possibly dormant virus activated by sunlight or infection.
Early symptoms:	'Butterfly' rash on nose and cheeks.
Course:	Joint pains, temperature, exhaustion.
Complications:	Damage to blood vessels, kidneys.
Treatment:	Painkillers, steroids, anti-malarial drugs.
Outlook:	Fair.
Prevention:	None known.
Gravity rating 3:	See also rheumatoid arthritis.

Common name:	**MANIC DEPRESSIVE PSYCHOSIS** ***A) Phase 1*** ***B) Phase 2***
Alternate name(s):	Cyclical insanity.
Cause:	Unknown.
Early symptoms:	Alternating elation (Phase 1) and depression (Phase 2).
Course:	Hyperactivity, talkativeness (Phase1) depresssion and withdrawal (Phase 2).
Complications:	Aggression (Phase 1); suicide (Phase 2).
Treatment:	Psychotropic drugs, ECT, family counselling.
Outlook:	Fair.
Prevention:	None known.
Gravity rating 3:	See also schizophrenia, depression.

Common name:	**MASTITIS**
Alternate name(s):	Breast inflammation, breast abscess.
Cause:	Infection usually after giving birth.
Early symptoms:	Tenderness on breast feeding.
Course:	Swelling, reddening, throbbing, temperature.
Complications:	Abscess forms, septicaemia.
Treatment:	Support, pain relief, antibiotics, draining.
Outlook:	Good.
Prevention:	Hygiene, adequate nutrition.
Gravity rating 1	

Common name:	**MASTOIDITIS**
Alternate name(s):	Infection of bone behind ear.
Cause:	Spread from middle ear infection.
Early symptoms:	Earache, ear noises, running ear.
Course:	Temperature, pain in bone, tender to touch, headache.
Complications:	Spread to brain, permanent deafness, chronic discharge.
Treatment:	Antibiotics, surgery.
Outlook:	Good.
Prevention:	Prompt treatment of ear infections.
Gravity rating 2:	See also earache.

Common name:	**MEASLES**
Alternate name(s):	Morbilli.
Cause:	Viral infection.
Early symptoms:	Running nose, cough.
Course:	Diffuse rash, sore eyes, headache.
Complications:	Pneumonia, ear infection, encephalitis.
Treatment:	Bed rest, light diet, cough mixture, antibiotics.
Outlook:	Good.
Prevention:	Vaccination, avoid contact with active case.

Gravity rating 2

Common name:	**MELANOMA**
Alternate name(s):	Malignant mole, pigmented naevus.
Cause:	Congenital in some cases.
Early symptoms:	Black growth on skin.
Course:	Increase in size.
Complications:	Spread.
Treatment:	Surgery, radiation, cytotoxic drugs.
Outlook:	Fair.
Prevention:	Avoid irritation of existing moles, surgery if at risk.
Gravity rating 4:	See also skin cancer.

Common name: **MÉNIÈRE'S DISEASE**
Alternate name(s): Labyrinthitis.
Cause: Fluid in inner ear, meningitis, injury, drug reaction.
Early symptoms: Dizziness, hearing changes, tinnitus.
Course: Headache, nausea, vomiting, falling.
Complications: Vision defects, injuries from falls.
Treatment: Cause if known, anti-vertigo drugs, low-salt diet, surgery, counselling.
Outlook: Fair.
Prevention: Removal of known cause.
Gravity rating 2: See also vertigo, otitis.

Common name: **MENINGITIS**
A) BACTERIAL MENINGITIS
Alternate name(s): Brain fever.
Cause: Bacterial infection of brain lining.
Early symptoms: Headache, temperature, nausea, vomiting.
Course: Bright light hurts, stiff neck, unconsciousness.
Complications: Permanent mental changes, deafness.
Treatment: Antibiotics.
Outlook: Fair.
Prevention: Vaccination, treatment of other infections, hygiene.
Gravity rating 3

B) TUBERCULOSIS MENINGITIS

Alternate name(s):	TBM.
Cause:	Tuberculous infection of brain lining.
Early symptoms:	Intermittent headache, nausea, temperature.
Course:	Symptoms become severe and persistent.
Complications:	Generalised spread.
Treatment:	Anti-tuberculosis drugs.
Outlook:	Fair.
Prevention:	Treatment of known tuberculous infections, BCG vaccination.
Gravity rating 4:	See also tuberculosis.

C) VIRAL MENINGITIS

Alternate name(s):	Benign meningitis.
Cause:	Viral infection of brain lining.
Early symptoms:	Headache, temperature, nausea.
Course:	Stiff neck.
Complications:	Deafness, brain damage.
Treatment:	Symptomatic.
Outlook:	Good.
Prevention:	Avoid contact with known cases.

Gravity rating 2

Common name:	**MENOPAUSE**
Alternate name(s):	Change of life, climacteric.
Cause:	Hormonal age changes.
Early symptoms:	Hot flushes, irritability, irregular periods.
Course:	Vaginal dryness, variable.
Complications:	Depression, osteoporosis later.
Treatment:	Hormone replacement, psychological support.
Outlook:	Good.
Prevention:	Education, counselling, early hormone therapy.
Gravity rating 2:	See also osteoporosis.

Common name:	**MENORRHAGIA**
Alternate name(s):	Heavy periods, flooding, prolonged periods.
Cause:	Fibroids, malignancies, hormone imbalance, psychic stress.
Early symptoms:	Excessive regular menstrual bleeding.
Course:	Severe blood loss.
Complications:	Anaemia.
Treatment:	Bed rest, investigation, hormones, surgery.
Outlook:	Good, unless malignant.
Prevention:	None known.
Gravity rating 2:	See also endometritis, fibroids, metrorrhagia.

Common name:	**METRORRHAGIA**
Alternate name(s):	Intermenstrual bleeding, spotting, irregular periods.
Cause:	Fibroids, uterine cancer, infection.
Early symptoms:	Spotting bleeding between periods or after menopause.
Course:	Heavier more prolonged bleeding.
Complications:	Malignancy, anaemia.
Treatment:	Investigation, surgery.
Outlook:	Good unless malignant.
Prevention:	None.
Gravity rating 2	See also menorrhagia, fibroids, endometritis.

Common name:	**MIGRAINE**
Alternate name(s):	Sick headache, recurrent headache, periodic headache.
Cause:	Raised blood pressure, arterio-sclerosis, allergy, tension, diet, alcohol, contraceptive pill, unknown.
Early symptoms:	Flickering lights, vision faults, nausea.
Course:	Headache, vomiting, shivering, irritability.
Complications:	Serious upset in work or pleasure, stroke.
Treatment:	Ergot type drugs, rest in dark.
Outlook:	Good.
Prevention:	Avoid known triggers, take special tablets regularly.

Gravity rating 2

Common name:	**MORNING SICKNESS**
Alternate name(s):	Pregnancy vomiting, hyperemesis gravidarum.
Cause:	Unknown, anxiety.
Early symptoms:	Morning nausea in first twelve weeks of pregnancy.
Course:	Usually settles in fourth month.
Complications:	Persistent severe vomiting, malnutrition, dehydration, underweight baby, abortion.
Treatment:	Light diet, rest, anti-vomiting drugs *with caution*, vitamins.
Outlook:	Good.
Prevention:	Light diet, pre-natal care.
Gravity rating 2	

Common name:	**MOTION SICKNESS**
Alternate name(s):	Travel, air, car, train, sea sickness.
Cause:	Irregular movment of vehicle, anxiety.
Early symptoms:	Nausea, dizziness.
Course:	Vomiting.
Complications:	Dehydration.
Treatment:	Anti-vomiting drugs.
Outlook:	Good.
Prevention:	Light diet, rest, fresh air, mild sedation, psychotherapy.
Gravity rating 1	

Common name:	**MULTIPLE SCLEROSIS**
Alternate name(s):	Disseminated sclerosis, MS.
Cause:	Unknown, possible viral damage to nerve coverings.
Early symptoms:	Very variable, transient double or blurred vision, weakness, clumsiness.
Course:	Slurred speech, incontinence.
Complications:	Paralysis.
Treatment:	Supportive and symptomatic, maintainence of general health, physiotherapy.
Outlook:	Poor.
Prevention:	None known.
Gravity rating 4	

Common name:	**MUMPS**
Alternate name(s):	Parotitis.
Cause:	Viral infection of parotoid gland(s).
Early symptoms:	Swelling of glands at angle of jaw, slight temperature.
Course:	General malaise.
Complications:	Spread to sex glands, sterility, deafness.
Treatment:	Relief of pain, fluids, steroids for complications.
Outlook:	Good.
Prevention:	Vaccination, avoid contact with case.
Gravity rating 1:	See also orchitis.

Common name:	**MUSCULAR DYSTROPHY**
Alternate name(s):	MD, muscle wasting.
Cause:	Hereditary.
Early symptoms:	Child becomes clumsy.
Course:	Muscles of pelvis, legs, shoulders become weak.
Complications:	Total paralysis, wheelchair life.
Treatment:	Symptomatic and supportive only.
Outlook:	Poor.
Prevention:	Genetic counselling before conception.
Gravity rating 5	

Common name:	**MYALGIC ENCEPHALOMYELITIS**
Alternate name(s):	ME, post-flu debility, yuppie flu.
Cause:	Viral infection.
Early symptoms:	Extreme fatigue, muscle pains, skin rash, headache.
Course:	Rigors, temperature, nausea, tinnitus, increasing frequency of urinating.
Complications:	Depression.
Treatment:	Supportive, rest, light nutritious diet, anti-depressants.
Outlook:	Variable.
Prevention:	Adequate treatment and convalescence for all viral diseases.
Gravity rating 3:	See also influenza.

Common name:	**MYELOMA**
Alternate name(s):	Bone marrow cancer.
Cause:	Unknown.
Early symptoms:	Aching bone pain, anaemia, weight loss.
Course:	Steady deterioration.
Complications:	Bone fractures, paraplegia, kidney failure.
Treatment:	Radiation, chemotherapy.
Outlook:	Poor.
Prevention:	None known.
Gravity rating 5:	See also cancer.

Common name:	**MYOCARDIAL INFARCT**
Alternate name(s):	Heart attack, coronary occlusion, coronary thrombosis.
Cause:	Sudden obstruction of hardened coronary artery.
Early symptoms:	Acute tight chest pain radiating to arm(s), neck, jaw, back.
Course:	Pale, sweating, faint pulse, collapse.
Complications:	Sudden death, long-term disability.
Treatment:	Rest, pain relief, oxygen, hospital.
Outlook:	Fair.
Prevention:	Weight loss, stop smoking, anti-clotting medicines, by-pass surgery.
Gravity rating 4:	See also angina, heart disease, coronary thrombosis.

Common name:	**MYOCARDITIS**
Alternate name(s):	Inflammation of heart muscle.
Cause:	Spread of viral or bacterial infection from elsewhere.
Early symptoms:	Temperature, excessive tiredness.
Course:	Breathlessness, original illness persisting, chest discomfort.
Complications:	Heart failure, chronic disability.
Treatment:	Rest, antibiotics, treatment of original infection.
Outlook:	Good.
Prevention:	Adequate treatment of infections.
Gravity rating 3:	See also endocarditis, heart disease.

Common name:	**NEPHRITIS**
Alternate name(s):	Kidney inflammation, Bright's disease.
Cause:	Streptococcal infection, toxic chemicals.
Early symptoms:	Puffiness of face and ankles.
Course:	Headache, temperature, breathlessness, scanty urine, blood in urine.
Complications:	Kidney and heart failure, coma, chronic infection.
Treatment:	Bed rest, antibiotics, diet, dialysis, renal transplant.
Outlook:	Fair.
Prevention:	Adequate treatment of streptococcal infections, avoid toxic chemicals.
Gravity rating 3	

Common name:	**NEURALGIA**
Alternate name(s):	Nerve pain.
Cause:	Multiple causes e.g. shingles, nerve injury, pressure on a nerve.
Early symptoms:	Severe pain along course of nerve.
Course:	Not appropriate.
Complications:	Becoming chronic, depression.
Treatment:	Find and remove cause, painkillers, nerve destruction.
Outlook:	Fair.
Prevention:	None known.
Gravity rating 2:	See also herpes, migraine, trigeminal neuralgia, shingles.

Common name:	**NEURITIS**
Alternate name(s):	Nerve inflammation.
Cause:	Chronic poisoning, alcoholism, vitamin B deficiency, chronic diseases, toxic chemicals.
Early symptoms:	Tingling, numbness.
Course:	Muscle wasting, dropped wrist or ankle.
Complications:	Permanent nerve damage, partial paralysis.
Treatment:	Stop cause, rest area, physiotherapy, vitamin B, steroids.
Outlook:	Good.
Prevention:	Avoid known causes.
Gravity rating 2:	See also Bell's palsy, trigeminal neuralgia, sciatica, shingles.

Common name:	**NOSE BLEED**
Alternate name(s):	Epistaxis.
Cause:	Injury, infection, tumour, head injury, blood pressure.
Early symptoms:	Flow of blood from nose.
Course:	Not appropriate.
Complications:	Anaemia.
Treatment:	Pinch nostrils together for 20 minutes, plugging, find cause.
Outlook:	Good.
Prevention:	Treat underlying cause.
Gravity rating 1:	See also haemophilia.

Common name:	**OESOPHAGEAL DIVERTICULUM**
Alternate name(s):	Pouch in the gullet.
Cause:	Congenital, repeated pressure, injury.
Early symptoms:	Excessive mucus, difficulty swallowing, halitosis.
Course:	Regurgitation of food, weight loss.
Complications:	Infection, perforation.
Treatment:	Surgery.
Outlook:	Good.
Prevention:	None.
Gravity rating 2	

Common name:	**OOPHORITIS**
Alternate name(s):	Ovarian infection.
Cause:	Bacterial infection, TB, mumps, gonorrhoea.
Early symptoms:	Low abdominal pain, nausea, tenderness, temperature.
Course:	Abscess develops.
Complications:	Rupture of abscess, peritonitis, internal scarring, sterility.
Treatment:	Antibiotics, surgery.
Outlook:	Fair.
Prevention:	Adequate treatment of original infection.

Gravity rating 2

Common name:	**ORCHITIS**
Alternate name:	Testicular inflammation.
Cause:	Mumps, TB, gonorrhoea, prostatic infection.
Early symptoms:	Testicle swollen and tender, temperature.
Course:	Shivering, malaise.
Complications:	Sterility.
Treatment:	Rest, elevation, painkillers, steroids, antibiotics.
Outlook:	Good.
Prevention:	Vaccination against mumps, avoid infected sexual partners.
Gravity rating 1:	See also mumps, tuberculosis.

Common name:	**OSTEOARTHRITIS**
Alternate name(s):	Degenerative joint disease.
Cause:	Joint damage from injury, overweight, ageing, poor posture.
Early symptoms:	Pain and stiffness.
Course:	Distortion of affected joint(s).
Complications:	Severe pain and immobility.
Treatment:	Pain relief, surgical replacement.
Outlook:	Progressive.
Prevention:	Avoid straining and injury, reduce weight.
Gravity rating 2:	See also arthritis, rheumatoid arthritis.

Common name:	**OSTEOMALACIA**
Alternate name(s):	Bone softening, adult rickets.
Cause:	Deficiency of calcium and vitamin D.
Early symptoms:	Aching bones.
Course:	Long bones bent, pelvis and vertebrae distorted.
Complications:	Progressive distortion, pressure on spinal cord, paralysis.
Treatment:	Vitamin D concentrate.
Outlook:	Fair.
Prevention:	Diet adequate in vitamin D.
Gravity rating 2:	See also vitamin deficiency, rickets.

Common name:	**OSTEOMYELITIS**
Alternate name(s):	Bone inflammation, infection.
Cause:	Injury involving bone, occasionally TB.
Early symptoms:	Severe localised pain, high temperature, shivering.
Course:	Area red, very tender, pus discharge.
Complications:	Becomes chronic, shortening and distortion of bone, joint involvement.
Treatment:	Antibiotics, pain relief, bed rest, surgery.
Outlook:	Fair.
Prevention:	Prevention and treatment of infections.

Gravity rating 3

Common name:	**OSTEOPOROSIS**
Alternate name(s):	Brittle bones.
Cause:	Hormonal changes, calcium loss.
Early symptoms:	Constant ache in bones.
Course:	Loss of stature, stooped posture.
Complications:	Fractures, severe deformities.
Treatment:	Splinting, exercises.
Outlook:	Progressive.
Prevention:	Hormone replacement at menopause.
Gravity rating 2:	See also kyphosis, menopause.

Common name:	**OTOSCLEROSIS**
Alternate name(s):	Middle ear hardening.
Cause:	Unknown.
Early symptoms:	Tinnitus.
Course:	Progressive deafness.
Complications:	Total deafness.
Treatment:	Surgery.
Outlook:	Fair.
Prevention:	None known.
Gravity rating 1:	See also tinnitus, earache, Ménière's disease.

Common name:	**PAGET'S DISEASE (BONE)**
Alternate name(s):	Osteitis deformans.
Cause:	Disturbance of bone metabolism, calcium loss.
Early symptoms:	Enlargement of skull, leg and spinal bones, bone pain.
Course:	Skeletal distortion.
Complications:	Spontaneous fractures, severe skeletal deformities.
Treatment:	Long-term injections.
Outlook:	Slowly progressive.
Prevention:	None known.
Gravity rating 3	

Common name:	**PAGET'S DISEASE (BREAST)**
Alternate name(s):	Paget's breast cancer.
Cause:	Unknown.
Early symptoms:	Red, dry, cracked nipples.
Course:	Tenderness, ulceration, discharge.
Complications:	Progress to cancer of body of breast.
Treatment:	Surgery with careful follow up.
Outlook:	Fair.
Prevention:	None known.
Gravity rating 3:	See also breast cancer.

Common name:	**PANCREATITIS (ACUTE)**
Alternate name(s):	Pancreatic inflammation.
Cause:	Alcoholism, liver disease, diabetes, peptic ulcer.
Early symptoms:	Nausea, vomiting, bloated feeling, abdominal pain.
Course:	Severe abdominal pain, shock.
Complications:	Haemorrhage, peritonitis, diabetes.
Treatment:	Antibiotics, pain relief, steroids, surgery.
Outlook:	Poor.
Prevention:	Moderation in eating and drinking, treatment of other abdominal conditions.
Gravity rating 4:	See also peritonitis, peptic ulcer, gall-bladder, cirrhosis.

Common name: **PARAPLEGIA**
Alternate name(s): Double leg paralysis, lower body paralysis.
Cause: Pressure on spinal cord from injury, tumour, infection, disc lesions.
Early symptoms: Pain and tingling in both legs.
Course: Complete bilateral paralysis.
Complications: Bladder infection, impotence, bedsores, depression.
Treatment: Removal of cause if possible, physiotherapy, supportive.
Outlook: Poor.
Prevention: Proper transport of spinal injuries, early treatment of sciatica, lumbago.
Gravity rating 4: See also disc lesion, sciatica, TB, kyphosis.

Common name: **PARKINSONISM**
Alternate name(s): Paralysis agitans, shaking palsy.
Cause: Viral infection, arterio-sclerosis, toxic absorption, injury, chemicals.
Early symptoms: Tremors in hands, general slowness, salivation.
Course: Loss of facial mobility, tottering gait, falling.
Complications: Mood changes, depression, social problems.
Treatment: Specific drugs, physio-therapy, surgery, speech therapy.
Outlook: Progressive.
Prevention: None known.
Gravity rating 3

Common name: **PELLAGRA**
Alternate name(s): Vitamin B3 deficiency, nicotinic acid deficiency.
Cause: Poor diet, alcoholism.
Early symptoms: Headache, confusion, loss of appetite, intestinal upset.
Course: Sore tongue, mouth and mucosa, skin rashes, ulcers.
Complications: Mental and physical deterioration.
Treatment: Nicotinic acid by mouth or injection, improved diet.
Outlook: Good.
Prevention: Supervision of diet in at-risk persons, aged, drop-outs, alcoholics, drug addicts.
Gravity rating 3: See also vitamins.

Common name: **PEPTIC ULCER (DUODENUM)**
Alternate name(s): Duodenal ulcer.
Cause: Stress, dietary faults, smoking, alcohol, excess acid.
Early symptoms: Discomfort 1–2 hours after meals.
Course: Abdominal pain, nausea, flatulence.
Complications: Haemorrhage, perforation.
Treatment: Rest, alkalies, acid-inhibiting drugs, anti-spasmodics, diet, surgery.
Outlook: Good.
Prevention: Relaxation, bland unhurried meals, no smoking or alcohol.
Gravity rating 2

Common name:	**PEPTIC ULCER (STOMACH)**
Alternate name(s):	Gastric ulcer.
Cause:	Stress, dietary indiscretion, excess acid.
Early symptoms:	Abdominal pain shortly after food.
Course:	Nausea, vomiting.
Complications:	Haemorrhage, perforation, malignant change.
Treatment:	Rest, antacids, acid-inhibiting drugs, diet, surgery, alkalies.
Outlook:	Good.
Prevention:	Relaxation, bland diet, no smoking or alcohol.

Gravity rating 2

Common name:	**PERICARDITIS**
Alternate name(s):	Inflammation of the outer lining of the heart.
Cause:	Bacterial infection from focus in body, injury, TB.
Early symptoms:	Chest pain, breathlessness, cough.
Course:	Swollen ankles, distended neck veins, enlarged liver.
Complications:	Cardiac failure.
Treatment:	Antibiotics, diuretics, rest, oxygen, pain relief.
Outlook:	Fair.
Prevention:	Early treatment of all infections.
Gravity rating 3:	See also heart failure.

Common name:	**PERITONITIS**
Alternate name(s):	Inflammation of internal abdominal lining.
Cause:	Ruptured internal organ, TB, injury.
Early symptoms:	Abdominal pain, vomiting.
Course:	Shock, collapse, abdominal distention.
Complications:	Haemorrhage, bowel paralysis.
Treatment:	Pain relief, no food, surgery, transfusion, antibiotics.
Outlook:	Fair.
Prevention:	Treatment of abdominal conditions.
Gravity rating 3:	See also peptic ulcer, gall-bladder, pancreatitis, appendicitis.

Common name:	**PHARYNGITIS**
Alternate name(s):	Inflammation of pharynx.
Cause:	Viral or bacterial infection, excessive smoking.
Early symptoms:	Sore throat, temperature, earache.
Course:	Swollen glands, difficulty in swallowing.
Complications:	Obstruction to breathing or swallowing.
Treatment:	Soothing applications, local antiseptics, antibiotics.
Outlook:	Good.
Prevention:	Avoid irritants, smoking, alcohol, fumes.
Gravity rating 1:	See also tonsillitis, croup, laryngitis.

Common name:	**PHLEBITIS**
Alternate name(s):	Inflamed vein.
Cause:	Infection, injury, varicosity.
Early symptoms:	Pain, throbbing, swelling.
Course:	Shivering, nausea, clotting, hard swelling.
Complications:	Embolism.
Treatment:	Anti-inflammatory drugs, anti-clotting drugs, rest, support.
Outlook:	Good.
Prevention:	Support of varicose veins, avoid injury to veins, exercise after surgery and childbirth.
Gravity rating 2:	See also varicose veins, thrombosis, embolism.

Common name:	**PILONIDAL CYST**
Alternate name(s):	Blocked sweat gland at base of spine.
Cause:	Ingrowing hairs block ducts.
Early symptoms:	Red swollen area.
Course:	Local abscess forms.
Complications:	Spread, chronic infection.
Treatment:	Drainage.
Outlook:	Good.
Prevention:	Local hygiene.
Gravity rating 1	

Common name:	**PITYRIASIS ROSEA**
Alternate name(s):	Not appropriate.
Cause:	Possibly virus.
Early symptoms:	Red patch on skin, slightly raised and scaly.
Course:	1-2 weeks later, similar clusters, slight itching.
Complications:	Rarely chronic.
Treatment:	Coal tar applications, ultra-violet light.
Outlook:	Good.
Prevention:	None known.
Gravity rating 0	

Common name:	**PLEURISY**
Alternate name(s):	Inflammation of lining of lung.
Cause:	Injury, clot, pneumonia, TB.
Early symptoms:	Sharp pain in chest made worse on breathing.
Course:	Temperature, patient lies on painful side.
Complications:	Pneumonia, empyema, bronchiectasis.
Treatment:	Antibiotics, pain relief, find cause, drainage of fluid.
Outlook:	Good.
Prevention:	Treatment of cause early.
Gravity rating 2:	See also pneumonia, devil's grip, empyema, bronchiectasis.

Common name:	**PNEUMOCONIOSIS**
Alternate name(s):	Miner's lung, farmer's lung, black spit, asbestosis, silicosis, anthracosis.
Cause:	Chronic lung inflammation due to inhaled dust or irritant.
Early symptoms:	Cough, coloured sputum.
Course:	Haemorrhage, infection, breathlessness.
Complications:	Emphysema, heart failure.
Treatment:	Remove from source of irritation, antibiotics, oxygen, physiotherapy, expectorant medicines.
Outlook:	Poor.
Prevention:	Proper working conditions, protective mask, ventilation.
Gravity rating 4:	See also emphysema, bronchiectasis.

Common name:	**PNEUMONIA**
Alternate name(s):	Lung consolidation.
Cause:	Infection, tumour, foreign body.
Early symptoms:	Shivering, cough, sharp chest pain, temperature.
Course:	Bloodstained sputum, panting, prostration.
Complications:	Lung abscess, heart failure, empyema.
Treatment:	Rest, supportive, antibiotics, fluids, pain relief.
Outlook:	Good.
Prevention:	Adequate treatment of respiratory infections.
Gravity rating 2:	See also bronchitis, pleurisy, empyema.

Common name:	**PNEUMOTHORAX**
Alternate name(s):	Collapsed lung.
Cause:	Injury, tumour, TB, excessive coughing.
Early symptoms:	Sudden breathlessness, chest pain.
Course:	Not appropriate.
Complications:	Heart failure.
Treatment:	Rest, re-inflation of lung, treat cause.
Outlook:	Good.
Prevention:	Prevent violent coughing, treat possible causes.
Gravity rating 2:	See also TB, bronchitis, lung cancer.

Common name:	**POLIOMYELITIS**
Alternate name(s):	Infantile paralysis, polio.
Cause:	Viral infection of spinal cord and brain.
Early symptoms:	Temperature, sore throat, nausea, headache.
Course:	Muscle pain and spasm, neck stiffness, severe headache.
Complications:	Paralysis of groups of muscles.
Treatment:	Rest, physiotherapy, assisted breathing.
Outlook:	Variable.
Prevention:	Vaccination, hygiene, sanitation.

Gravity rating 4

Common name:	**POST–NATAL DEPRESSION**
Alternate name(s):	Baby blues, puerperal depression.
Cause:	Hormone changes, environmental, anxiety.
Early symptoms:	Crying, feelings of anxiety and discouragement, over-tiredness after giving birth.
Course:	Mildly anti-social, withdrawn.
Complications:	Severe depressive psychosis, aggression towards husband or baby.
Treatment:	Reassurance, advice, general support, anti-depressive drugs.
Outlook:	Good.
Prevention:	Pre-natal education and counselling.
Gravity rating 1	

Common name:	**PRE-MENSTRUAL TENSION**
Alternate name(s):	PMT.
Cause:	Hormone changes, fluid retention.
Early symptoms:	Weight gain, headaches, irritability, insomnia, depression.
Course:	Enlargement of breasts, tender breasts.
Complications:	Marital friction.
Treatment:	Diuretics, vitamin B6, emotional support.
Outlook:	Good.
Prevention:	Diuretics before period, hormones.
Gravity rating 1:	See also dysmenorrhoea.

Common name:	**PROSTATIC SYNDROME**
Alternate name(s):	Old man's disease, benign prostatic hypertrophy.
Cause:	Swelling of prostate from 60 years onwards.
Early symptoms:	Increasing frequency of urination, getting up at night, poor control.
Course:	Incontinence, retention of urine.
Complications:	Cancerous change.
Treatment:	Surgery, hormones, steroids, catheterisation.
Outlook:	Fair.
Prevention:	None known.
Gravity rating 3:	See also prostatic cancer.

Common name:	**PSITTACOSIS**
Alternate name(s):	Parrot disease, ornithosis.
Cause:	Viral infection from birds.
Early symptoms:	Cough, slight temperature, sore throat.
Course:	Pneumonia, high temperature, headache, rash.
Complications:	Myocarditis.
Treatment:	Antibiotics.
Outlook:	Fair.
Prevention:	Avoid inhaling dust from bird cages when cleaning.
Gravity rating 3:	See also myocarditis.

Common name:	**PSORIASIS**
Alternate name(s):	Scaly skin.
Cause:	Hereditary, injury or infection may precipitate.
Early symptoms:	Silvery scales on red plaques mainly on knees and elbows.
Course:	Nails and scalp involved, sometimes whole body.
Complications:	Arthritis, depression.
Treatment:	Steroids, local application, ultra-violet light.
Outlook:	Variable.
Prevention:	None known.
Gravity rating 2:	See also rheumatoid arthritis.

Common name:	**PUERPERAL SEPSIS**
Alternate name(s):	Childbed fever.
Cause:	Infection during labour.
Early symptoms:	Abdominal discomfort.
Course:	Temperature, shivering, foul vaginal discharge.
Complications:	Septicaemia, peritonitis.
Treatment:	Antibiotics.
Outlook:	Good.
Prevention:	Asepsis before, during and after delivery.
Gravity rating 3:	See also septicaemia.

Common name:	**PULMONARY HEART DISEASE**
Alternate name(s):	Cor pulmonale.
Cause:	Heart enlargement due to lung disease.
Early symptoms:	Cough, breathlessness, wheezing, tiredness.
Course:	Swollen ankles, distended neck veins, tenderness over liver.
Complications:	Confusion, coma, convulsions.
Treatment:	Treat lung condition, low-salt diet, diuretics, oxygen.
Outlook:	Poor.
Prevention:	Treat lung conditions thoroughly.
Gravity rating 4:	See also bronchiectasis, emphysema, heart.

Common name:	**PURPURA**
Alternate name(s):	Petechiae.
Cause:	Multiple causes, should always be investigated.
Early symptoms:	Small round flat purple or red spots on skin.
Course:	Joint haemorrhages.
Complications:	Depends on underlying disease.
Treatment:	Depends on underlying disease, steroids, transfusion.
Outlook:	Variable.
Prevention:	Avoid drugs or radiation except under medical control.
Gravity rating 3:	See also leukaemia, allergy, scurvy.

Common name:	**PYELITIS**
Alternate name:	Kidney pelvis infection, UTI.
Cause:	Spread from focus in body.
Early symptoms:	Shivering, frequency of urination, temperature.
Course:	Abdominal pain, backache, pus in urine.
Complications:	Chronic infection, kidney damage.
Treatment:	Rest, warmth, fluids, antibiotics.
Outlook:	Good.
Prevention:	Adequate treatment of infections elsewhere.
Gravity rating 2:	See also nephritis.

Common name:	**PYORRHOEA**
Alternate name(s):	Gum infection.
Cause:	Poor dental hygiene, deficient diet.
Early symptoms:	Bleeding gums.
Course:	Obvious pus, halitosis.
Complications:	Loss of teeth, poor nutrition.
Treatment:	Mouth hygiene, dental care.
Outlook:	Good.
Prevention:	Regular dental care, mouth hygiene, adequate diet.
Gravity rating 1	

Common name:	**RABIES**
Alternate name(s):	Hydrophobia.
Cause:	Viral infection spread by rabid animals.
Early symptoms:	Agitation, restlessness after bite or lick on broken skin from infected animal.
Course:	Muscle spasms, convulsions.
Complications:	Paralysis of breathing muscles.
Treatment:	Anti-rabies serum, pain relief, sedation.
Outlook:	Poor.
Prevention:	Quarantine of imported animals, vaccination of persons at risk and pets in infected areas.

Gravity rating 5

Common name:	**RAYNAUD'S DISEASE**
Alternate name(s):	Paroxysmal digital cyanosis.
Cause:	Spasm of limb blood vessels due to cold, other diseases.
Early symptoms:	Fingers and toes become blue, cold, white, numb.
Course:	Painful ulceration.
Complications:	Superficial gangrene.
Treatment:	Keep extremities warm, treat any underlying condition, vasodilator drugs.
Outlook:	Variable.
Prevention:	Warmth, avoidance of stress.
Gravity rating 2:	See also Buerger's disease, scleroderma.

Common name: **RETINITIS PIGMENTOSA**
Alternate name(s): RP.
Cause: Hereditary defect of retina.
Early symptoms: Night blindness.
Course: Tunnel vision.
Complications: Progressive loss of sight, depression.
Treatment: None.
Outlook: Poor.
Prevention: Genetic counselling before conception.

Gravity rating 4

Common name: **RHEUMATIC FEVER**
Alternate name(s): Acute rheumatism.
Cause: Streptococcal infection.
Early symptoms: Sore throat, temperature, pains moving irregularly from joint to joint and muscle to muscle.
Course: Sweating, rapid pulse, malaise.
Complications: Heart and kidney damage.
Treatment: Strict rest, antibiotics, anti-inflammatory drugs, steroids.
Outlook: Good.
Prevention: Treatment of streptococcal infections.
Gravity rating 3: See also endocarditis.

Common name:	**RHEUMATOID ARTHRITIS**
Alternate name(s):	RA, rheumatoid disease.
Cause:	Breakdown of body's self-defence system.
Early symptoms:	Redness and swelling around small joints, pain, fever.
Course:	Nodules and distortion of joints, muscle wasting.
Complications:	Heart and lung involvement, diabetes, anaemia, psoriasis.
Treatment:	Pain relief, steroids, gold injections, physiotherapy, corrective surgery.
Outlook:	Fair.
Prevention:	None known.
Gravity rating 4:	See also lupus erythematosis, synovitis, psoriasis.

Common name:	**RICKETS**
Alternate name(s):	Vitamin D deficiency.
Cause:	Poor diet, lack of sunlight.
Early symptoms:	Infant growth delayed, bones soft and distorted.
Course:	Swollen abdomen, diarrhoea, anaemia.
Complications:	Infections, permanent bone distortion, kyphosis.
Treatment:	Vitamin D concentrate, sunlight, surgical correction for deformities.
Outlook:	Good.
Prevention:	Adequate vitamin D in diet, sunlight.
Gravity rating 2:	See also osteomalacia.

Common name: **RINGWORM**
Alternate name(s): Tinea infection, jock itch.
Cause: Fungal skin infection.
Early symptoms: Slight itch on scalp or body, small scaly spots, hair loss.
Course: Not appropriate.
Complications: Secondary infection with scarring.
Treatment: Griseofulvin by mouth, local applications, hygiene.
Outlook: Good.
Prevention: No exchange of clothing, personal hygiene, clean combs, hairbrushes.
Gravity rating 0: See also athlete's foot.

Common name: **ROUNDWORM**
Alternate name(s): *Ascaris lumbricoides* infestation.
Cause: Consuming infected food.
Early symptoms: Abdominal pain, diarrhoea, loss of appetite.
Course: Worm(s) passed or vomited.
Complications: Severe malnutrition, intestinal obstruction, pneumonia.
Treatment: Special roundworm killing drugs.
Outlook: Good.
Prevention: Adequate cooking of food, hygiene.
Gravity rating 2: See also threadworm, tapeworm.

Common name:	**SARCOIDOSIS**
Alternate name(s):	Boeck's sarcoid.
Cause:	Unknown.
Early symptoms:	Cough, weight loss, fatigue.
Course:	Enlargement of liver, spleen, glands.
Complications:	Eye, heart or nerve involvement.
Treatment:	Steroids, chloroquine.
Outlook:	Fair.
Prevention:	None known.
Gravity rating 3	

Common name:	**SCABIES**
Alternate name(s):	The itch, sarcoptic mange.
Cause:	Skin infection with sarcoptic organism.
Early symptoms:	Skin irritation.
Course:	Linear scratches, intense itching.
Complications:	Secondary infection, eczematous changes.
Treatment:	Anti-scabetic lotions, change of clothing.
Outlook:	Good.
Prevention:	Good personal hygiene.
Gravity rating 0:	See also eczema, impetigo.

Common name: **SCARLET FEVER**
Alternate name(s): Scarlatina.
Cause: Streptococcal infection.
Early symptoms: Sore throat, temperature, joint pains.
Course: Diffuse fine red rash
Complications: Kidney and heart infection.
Treatment: Rest, antibiotics.
Outlook: Good.
Prevention: Adequate control of sore throats and other infections.

Gravity rating 2

Common name: **SCHISTOSOMIASIS**
Alternate name(s): Bilharzia.
Cause: Flatworm infestation from bathing in contaminated water.
Early symptoms: Skin irritation.
Course: Temperature, diarrhoea, colic, tiredness, swollen abdomen.
Complications: Gross enlargement of liver and spleen, anaemia, urinary damage, vomiting blood, brain damage.
Treatment: Specific medicines.
Outlook: Fair.
Prevention: Public hygiene and sanitation, care about bathing places.

Gravity rating 4

Common name:	**SCHIZOPHRENIA**
Alternate name(s):	Split personality, dementia praecox.
Cause:	Unknown, possibly hereditary.
Early symptoms:	Alternating depression and excitement, social withdrawal.
Course:	Suspicion, delusions of persecution or grandeur, hallucinations.
Complications:	Violence to others.
Treatment:	Psychotropic drugs, ECT, psychotherapy.
Outlook:	Fair.
Prevention:	None known.
Gravity rating 3:	See also manic depression.

Common name:	**SCIATICA**
Alternate name(s):	Sciatic neuritis.
Cause:	Inflammation, infection, pressure, injury, disc lesion.
Early symptoms:	Tingling pain along course of sciatic nerve.
Course:	Severe pain, limping, disability.
Complications:	Paralysis, transient or permanent.
Treatment:	Treat cause, rest, painkillers, relaxants, physiotherapy.
Outlook:	Good, depends on cause.
Prevention:	Avoid sudden strains, poor posture.
Gravity rating 2:	See also lumbago, slipped disc, neuritis, neuralgia.

Common name:	**SCLERODERMA**
Alternate name(s):	Hidebound skin, progressive systemic sclerosis.
Cause:	Possible allergy, hereditary, toxaemia.
Early symptoms:	Skin hard and thickened, circulation poor.
Course:	General rigidity, ulceration, arthritis.
Complications:	Pneumonia, heart and kidney failure, internal organs damaged.
Treatment:	Symptomatic and supportive.
Outlook:	Poor.
Prevention:	None known.
Gravity rating 5:	See also Raynaud's disease.

Common name:	**SCURVY**
Alternate name(s):	Vitamin C deficiency.
Cause:	Defective diet, improper cooking of vegetables, infections.
Early symptoms:	Bleeding gums, irritability, joint swelling (in infants).
Course:	Internal haemorrhage, weight loss, tooth loss.
Complications:	Severe anaemia, heart, lung, bone marrow damage.
Treatment:	Vitamin C concentrates, fresh fruit, raw vegetables.
Outlook:	Good.
Prevention:	Adequate diet, no use of bread soda in cooking vegetables.
Gravity rating 2:	See also vitamins.

Common name: **SEBORRHOEA**
Alternate name(s): Seborrhoeic dermatitis, oily skin.
Cause: Excess oily sweat, probably hormonal effect.
Early symptoms: Itching, greasy skin, scaly dandruff.
Course: Reddening, fissuring of skin.
Complications: Secondary infection.
Treatment: Bland non-irritant diet, locally applied creams, personal hygiene.
Outlook: May become chronic.
Prevention: None known, avoid stress, constipation, infections.
Gravity rating 1

Common name: **SEPTICAEMIA**
Alternate name(s): Blood poisoning, bacteraemia.
Cause: Microbes spread from local infection such as, sore throat or a boil into the blood stream where they grow.
Early symptoms: Shivering, temperature.
Course: Headache, collapse, muscle and joint pain.
Complications: Involvement of heart and other vital organs.
Treatment: Antibiotics, blood transfusion.
Outlook: Fair.
Prevention: Treatment of local infections.
Gravity rating 3: See also endocarditis.

Common name:	**SHINGLES**
Alternate name(s):	Zona, herpes zoster.
Cause:	Viral infection of nerve(s).
Early symptoms:	Pain along course of nerve(s).
Course:	Blisters along same area.
Complications:	Permanent pain, scarring, eye involvement.
Treatment:	Anti-viral paint and tablets, painkillers.
Outlook:	Good.
Prevention:	Elderly people avoid children with chickenpox.
Gravity rating 1:	See also neuritis, neuralgia.

Common name:	**SINUSITIS**
Alternate name(s):	Sinus headache.
Cause:	Infection of nasal sinuses, cold, irritants.
Early symptoms:	Frontal headache, throbbing.
Course:	Temperature, severe head-ache, discharge of mucopus.
Complications:	Chronic, spread to brain, ear involvement.
Treatment:	Warmth, antibiotics, surgical drainage, no swimming or flying until recovery is complete.
Outlook:	Good.
Prevention:	Treat colds, avoid irritants and local chilling.
Gravity rating 2	

Common name:	**'SLIPPED' DISC**
Alternate name(s):	Disc lesion, prolapsed disc, herniated disc.
Cause:	Sudden strain or pressure injuring pads between vertebrae.
Early symptoms:	Pain in neck or back radiating to arms and legs.
Course:	Stiffness, numbness and tingling.
Complications:	Paralysis, chronic pain and disability.
Treatment:	Rest, physiotherapy, anti-spasmodics, pain relief, surgery.
Outlook:	Fair.
Prevention:	Lifting and bending properly.
Gravity rating 2:	See also lumbago, whip lash, sciatica.

Common name:	**SPINA BIFIDA**
Alternate name(s):	Split spine.
Cause:	Failure of vertebra(e) to fuse centrally, genetic, possibly infection of mother in early pregnancy.
Early symptoms:	Open or closed swelling over lower backbone noted at or shortly after birth.
Course:	Paralysis, incontinence.
Complications:	Exposure of spinal cord, ulceration, infection.
Treatment:	Surgery, symptomatic, social and psychological support.
Outlook:	Chronic.
Prevention:	Genetic counselling before conception.
Gravity rating 4:	See also hydrocephalus.

Common name:	**SQUINT**
Alternate name(s):	Turned eye, strabismus, wall eye, cock-eye, lazy eye.
Cause:	Congenital, injury, nerve infection.
Early symptoms:	Eye(s) turned inwards or outwards.
Course:	Distortion increases, double vision.
Complications:	Loss of vision on one side.
Treatment:	Covering good eye, surgery, exercises, glasses.
Outlook:	Good.
Prevention:	Not appropriate.
Gravity rating 1	

Common name:	**STILL'S DISEASE**
Alternate name(s):	Juvenile rheumatoid arthritis.
Cause:	Breakdown in body's self-defence mechanism before the age of sixteen years.
Early symptoms:	Temperature, rash.
Course:	One or more joints inflamed and painful.
Complications:	Eye, spleen, liver, heart damage, chronic deformity, depression.
Treatment:	Rest, pain relief, steroids, physiotherapy, social support.
Outlook:	Poor.
Prevention:	None known.
Gravity rating 4:	See also iritis, rheumatoid arthritis.

Common name:	**STROKE**
Alternate name(s):	Apoplexy, CVA, cerebro-vascular accident.
Cause:	Brain blood supply cut off by
	A. Thrombosis.
	B. Embolus.
	C. Haemorrhage.

A) THROMBOSIS

Early symptoms:	Dizziness, slurred speech, amnesia.
Course:	One-sided paralysis, speech loss, unconsciousness.
Complications:	Pneumonia, urinary infection, incomplete recovery.
Treatment:	Anti-clotting drugs, physiotherapy, re-education.
Outlook:	Fair.
Prevention:	Small regular doses of anti-clotting drugs in person at risk.
Gravity rating 3:	See also thrombosis, arteriosclerosis.

B) EMBOLUS

Early symptoms:	Sudden paralysis, loss of speech.
Course:	Unconsciousness.
Complications:	Pneumonia, secondary tumour growth.
Treatment:	Life support, physiotherapy, re-education.
Outlook:	Fair.
Prevention:	Treatment of phlebitis, valvular heart disease, tumours.
Gravity rating 3:	See also endocarditis, phlebitis, cancer, embolism.

C) *HAEMORRHAGE*

Early symptoms:	Dizziness, slurred speech, headache.
Course:	Unconsciousness, paralysis.
Complications:	Pneumonia, permanent disability.
Treatment:	Life support, rest, re-education, physiotherapy.
Outlook:	Fair.
Prevention:	Lower blood pressure, avoid sudden stress and exertion.
Gravity rating 3:	See also high blood pressure.

Common name:	**STYE**
Alternate name(s):	Eyelid abscess.
Cause:	Infection of eyelid gland.
Early symptoms:	Small red patch, mild irritation.
Course:	Abscess forms.
Complications:	Recurrent infection, spread to eye surface.
Treatment:	Local antibiotics, heat, drainage.
Outlook:	Good.
Prevention:	Personal hygiene, no shared towels or face cloths.
Gravity rating 1:	See also blepharitis, trachoma.

Common name:	**SUBARACHNOID HAEMORRHAGE**
Alternate name(s):	Not appropriate.
Cause:	Bleeding between two layers of brain coverings.
Early symptoms:	Severe sudden headache.
Course:	Dizziness, vomiting, transient unconsciousness, neck stiffness, convulsions.
Complications:	Coma, death.
Treatment:	Rest, pain relief in some cases, reduce blood pressure, surgery sometimes, physiotherapy.
Outlook:	Fair.
Prevention:	Reduce raised blood pressure, surgery sometimes.
Gravity rating 4:	See also aneurysm, blood pressure.

Common name:	**SYNOVITIS**
Alternate name(s):	Inflammation of joint capsule.
Cause:	Injury, inflammation.
Early symptoms:	Joint(s) tender, movements limited.
Course:	Swelling, severe pain, loss of mobility.
Complications:	Adhesions leading to stiffness.
Treatment:	Rest, anti-inflammatory drugs, physiotherapy.
Outlook:	Good.
Prevention:	Avoid joint injury or overuse.
Gravity rating 2:	See also rheumatism, bursitis.

Common name:	**SYPHILIS**
Alternate name(s):	The great pox, lues.
Cause:	Sexually transmitted infection, rarely accidental.
Early symptoms:	Painless sore on genitals or lips, rarely elsewhere.
Course:	Generalised rash, internal organs involved up to 20 years later if untreated.
Complications:	Damage to blood vessels, brain, liver, heart, bones.
Treatment:	Penicillin in large doses, other antibiotics.
Outlook:	Fair.
Prevention:	Avoid infected sexual partners, self protection, use of condoms.
Gravity rating 3:	See also AIDS, gonorrhoea, herpes, trichomoniasis.

Common name:	**TAPEWORM**
Alternate name(s):	Cestode, taenia.
Cause:	Infestation from uncooked beef, pork, fish.
Early symptoms:	Mild abdominal pain, nausea, bowel disturbance.
Course:	Segments of worm seen in motion.
Complications:	Invasion of heart, muscles, brain and eyes, obstruction, anaemia.
Treatment:	Vermifuge medicines.
Outlook:	Good.
Prevention:	Food hygiene, ensure adequate cooking of meat and fish.
Gravity rating 2:	See also roundworm, threadworm, trichinosis.

Common name: **TETANUS**
Alternate name(s): Lockjaw.
Cause: Infection with tetanus germ.
Early symptoms: Small wound remains sore and inflamed.
Course: Irritability, stiff neck, muscle spasms, difficulty swallowing.
Complications: Cardiac failure, asphyxsia.
Treatment: Sedation, anti-tetanus vaccine, antibiotics, oxygen.
Outlook: Poor.
Prevention: Routine vaccination, tetanus anti-toxin for injuries, clean wounds.

Gravity rating 5

Common name: **THREADWORM**
Alternate name(s): Pin worms, nematodes, enterobiasis.
Cause: Infestation from dust, contaminated foods, animals.
Early symptoms: Itching around anus and perineum at night.
Course: Worms seen in motions or on underclothes.
Complications: Possibly appendicitis.
Treatment: Vermifuges, scrupulous personal hygiene, change underclothing.
Outlook: Good.
Prevention: Personal hygiene, no dry-dusting of floors.
Gravity rating 0: See also roundworm, tapeworm, trichinosis.

Common name:	**THROMBOSIS**
	A) ARTERIAL THROMBOSIS
Alternate name(s):	Clotting.
Cause:	Arterio-sclerosis, pressure, injury, inflammation.
Early symptoms:	Pain, numbness, tingling arm or leg, limping.
Course:	Severe disability, pulse cannot be felt.
Complications:	Gangrene.
Treatment:	Relief of pain, anti-clotting drugs, surgery.
Outlook:	Fair.
Prevention:	Small regular doses of anti-clotting drugs, by-pass surgery.
Gravity rating 4:	See also heart attack, coronary, stroke, gangrene.
	B) VENOUS THROMBOSIS
Alternate name(s):	Thrombo-phlebitis, milk leg.
Cause:	Clotting in a vein usually in a leg.
Early symptoms:	Local swelling and pain in leg often after childbirth.
Course:	Swelling extends, shivering, temperature.
Complications:	Embolus involving vital organ.
Treatment:	Elastic support, anti-clotting drugs, anti-inflammatory drugs, supervised exercise.
Outlook:	Good.
Prevention:	Passive and active movement after childbirth and operations.
Gravity rating 2:	See also phlebitis, embolus, varicose veins.

Common name: **TINNITUS**
Alternate name(s): Ringing in the ears.
Cause: Unknown, ear irritation, age deterioration, raised blood pressure, Ménière's disease, wax, drugs.
Early symptoms: Ringing, buzzing, whistling in ear(s).
Course: Hearing diminishes.
Complications: Psychological stress, deafness.
Treatment: Removal of cause if found, 'masking' noise appliance.
Outlook: Progressive.
Prevention: None known.
Gravity rating 1: See also blood pressure, Ménière's disease.

Common name: **TONSILLITIS**
Alternate name(s): Sore throat, quinsy, peritonsillar abscess.
Cause: Infection in and around tonsils.
Early symptoms: Sore throat, painful swallowing, temperature.
Course: Abscess forms.
Complications: Obstruction to breathing and swallowing, infection spreads.
Treatment: Bed rest, fluids, antibiotics, pain relief, drainage of abscess surgically.
Outlook: Good.
Prevention: Early treatment of sore throats.
Gravity rating 2: See also pharyngitis, croup.

Common name: **TOXOPLASMOSIS**
Alternate name(s): Not appropriate.
Cause: Parasitic infection from animals, occasionally congenital.
Early symptoms: Sore throat, swollen glands, temperature.
Course: Rash.
Complications: Damage to liver, eye, heart, lung, brain damage in baby born to infected mother.
Treatment: Specific drugs and antibiotics.
Outlook: Fair.
Prevention: Care when cleaning animal excreta areas, wash vegetables, avoid raw or rare meat.
Gravity rating 3

Common name: **TRACHOMA**
Alternate name(s): Granular conjunctivitis.
Cause: Infection of inside of eyelid.
Early symptoms: Lids congested and swollen, light hurts, tears.
Course: Granular swelling on lids.
Complications: Corneal ulceration, blindness, lid distortion.
Treatment: Local antibiotics, surgery for scarring.
Outlook: Fair.
Prevention: Good ocular hygiene.
Gravity rating 2: See also conjunctivitis, blepharitis.

Common name: **TRENCH MOUTH**
Alternate name(s): Vincent's angina.
Cause: Infection of mouth and gums.
Early symptoms: Painful ulcers on gums, sore throat, halitosis.
Course: Temperature, metallic taste, ear pain, swollen glands.
Complications: Pyorrhoea, tooth loss.
Treatment: Mouth hygiene, antibiotics.
Outlook: Good.
Prevention: General nutrition, mouth hygiene.

Gravity rating 1

Common name: **TRICHINOSIS**
Alternate name(s): Pork roundworm, trichinella spiralis.
Cause: Eating inadequately cooked pork.
Early symptoms: Abdominal cramps, nausea, diarrhoea.
Course: Temperature, shivering, muscle pains, sore eyes, oedema.
Complications: Pneumonia, heart and brain involvement.
Treatment: Specific drug (thiabendazole).
Outlook: Fair.
Prevention: Proper preparation of pork.
Gravity rating 2: See also roundworm, tapeworm.

Common name:	**TRICHOMONIASIS**
Alternate name(s):	Parasitic sexual infection.
Cause:	Sexual contact.
Early symptoms:	Pain on urination, severe itching.
Course:	Ulceration, vaginal discharge, scrotal rash.
Complications:	Secondary infection, haemorrhage.
Treatment:	Anti-parasitic medication, for both partners.
Outlook:	Good.
Prevention:	Avoid infected partners, hygiene, circumcision in male, use of condoms.
Gravity rating 2:	See also AIDS, syphilis, gonorrhoea, herpes.

Common name:	**TRIGEMINAL NEURALGIA**
Alternate name(s):	*Tic douloureux.*
Cause:	Inflammation of trigeminal nerve in face.
Early symptoms:	Acute stabbing facial pain.
Course:	Tends to become chronic, intermittent.
Complications:	Depression.
Treatment:	Vitamin B12, anti-epileptic drugs, surgery, anti-depressive drugs.
Outlook:	May diminish in later years.
Prevention:	None, avoid cold draughts to face.
Gravity rating 2:	See also neuralgia.

Common name: **TUBERCULOSIS**
Alternate name(s): Consumption, TB, the white plague, phthisis, Koch's infection.
Cause: Infection with tuberculosis germs.

Tuberculosis may involve practically any part of the body and spread from a primary focus, most commonly in the lungs, to other organs, prevention hinges on good sanitation and nutrition. Pasteurisation of milk, BCG vaccination of infants, regular screening and thorough treatment of known cases and follow up checks of their associates. The main features of infection of various organs are summarised below.

Site: **BONE AND JOINT**
Alternate name(s): Not appropriate.
Cause: Often related to unpasteurised milk in undeveloped areas.
Early symptoms: Pain in affected area, sudden night pains, temperature.
Course: Progressive stiffness and disability.
Complications: Permanent deformity, stiff joint, hunchback.
Treatment: Rest, anti-tuberculosis drugs, surgery.
Outlook: Fair.
Prevention: Pasteurisation of milk, farm hygiene.
Gravity rating 3: See also kyphosis.

Site:	**BRAIN AND MENINGES**
Alternate name(s):	TB, meningitis, TBM.
Cause:	Spread from other focus in body.
Early symptoms:	Intermittent headache, irritability, temperature, loss of appetite.
Course:	Neck rigidity, vomiting, unconsciousness.
Complications:	Permanent mental and physical signs of brain damage.
Treatment:	Anti-tuberculosis drugs, rest, symptomatic.
Outlook:	Fair.
Prevention:	Treatment of tuberculosis elsewhere.
Gravity rating 4:	See also meningitis.

Site:	**INTESTINES**
Alternate name(s):	TB, enterocolitis.
Cause:	Spread from infected lungs.
Early symptoms:	Nausea, loss of appetite, flatulence, cramps.
Course:	Weight loss, diarrhoea or constipation.
Complications:	Anal fistula, intestinal obstruction, adhesions.
Treatment:	Anti-tuberculosis drugs, rest, surgery.
Outlook:	Fair.
Prevention:	Adequate treatment of lung TB.

Gravity rating 3

Site: ***KIDNEY***
Alternate name(s):   Genito-urinary TB.
Cause: Spread usually from lung.
Early symptoms: Frequency of urination, temperature, fatigue.
Course: Blood in urine, spread to bladder and sex organs.
Complications: Generalised infection, permanent kidney damage.
Treatment: Anti-tuberculosis drugs, rest, surgery.
Outlook: Fair.
Prevention: Adequate treatment of primary focus.
Gravity rating 3:   See also Addison's disease, orchitis.

Site: ***LUNGS***
Alternate name(s):   Phthisis, consumption, Koch's infection, the white plague.
Cause: Spread from active case by coughing, spitting, sneezing.
Early symptoms: Cough, tiredness, temperature in evening, breathlessness.
Course: Night sweats, chest pain, loss of appetite, blood in spit.
Complications: Destruction of lung, spread to other areas.
Treatment: Rest, anti-tuberculosis drugs.
Outlook: Good.
Prevention: Good sanitation, personal hygiene, BCG vaccination.

Gravity rating 3

Site: **LYMPH GLANDS**
Alternate name(s): Tuberculous adenopathy.
Cause: Spread from lungs to elsewhere.
Early symptoms: Swollen, slightly tender glands in neck or abdomen.
Course: Glands break down and ulcerate.
Complications: Generalised infection.
Treatment: Anti-tuberculosis drugs, surgery.
Outlook: Good.
Prevention: Adequate treatment of primary focus.

Gravity rating 2

Common name: **TYPHOID**
Alternate name(s): Enteric fever.
Cause: Food contaminated with typhoid germ from sewage.
Early symptoms: Headache, malaise, temperature, sore throat.
Course: Diarrhoea, vomiting, rash on abdomen and back, delirium.
Complications: Bowel perforation, pneumonia, chronic carrier state.
Treatment: Antibiotics, bed rest, symptomatic.
Outlook: Good.
Prevention: Vaccination of travellers, good hygiene and sanitation.
Gravity rating 3: See also gastro-enteritis, cholera.

Common name: **TYPHUS**
Alternate name(s): Gaol fever.
Cause: Infection from bite of infected louse, flea or tick.
Early symptoms: Severe headache, joint pains, temperature.
Course: High temperature, delirium.
Complications: Kidney and heart failure, pneumonia, skin gangrene.
Treatment: Antibiotics.
Outlook: 20% mortality.
Prevention: Vaccination, good personal hygiene, insect repellents.

Gravity rating 4

Common name: **ULCERATIVE COLITIS**
Alternate name(s): Chronic large bowel inflammation.
Cause: Possible allergy, body self-defence breaks down.
Early symptoms: Intermittent bloody diarrhoea, lower abdominal pain.
Course: Weight loss, anaemia, faecal incontinence, abdominal swelling.
Complications: Bowel abscess, obstruction, perforation, malignant change.
Treatment: Bed rest, full investigation, steroids, bowel disinfection, enemas, surgery.
Outlook: Poor.
Prevention: None known.
Gravity rating 4: See also cancer, colitis, Crohn's disease, incontinence.

Common name:	**URAEMIA**
Alternate name(s):	Raised blood urea.
Cause:	Infection or injury to kidney, urinary obstruction.
Early symptoms:	Reduced urinary output, headache, thirst.
Course:	Confusion, coma.
Complications:	Total kidney failure.
Treatment:	Increase urine output, dialysis, kidney transplant.
Outlook:	Poor.
Prevention:	Treatment of kidney, heart, prostate and other organ conditions.
Gravity rating 4:	See also nephritis, prostatic syndrome.

Common name:	**URETHRITIS**
Alternate name(s):	Urinary passage infection.
Cause:	Usually sexual contact.
Early symptoms:	Stinging pain passing water, frequency.
Course:	Pus in urine, shivering, temperature.
Complications:	Spread, later urinary obstruction.
Treatment:	Antibiotics.
Outlook:	Good.
Prevention:	Avoid infected sexual partners.
Gravity rating 2:	See also gonorrhoea.

Common name:	**VARICOSE VEINS**
Alternate name(s):	Swollen leg veins.
Cause:	Standing, obesity, pregnancy, hereditary.
Early symptoms:	Veins prominent, legs tired and heavy feeling.
Course:	Ulceration, swelling of ankles, infection.
Complications:	Haemorrhage, thrombosis, emboli.
Treatment:	Support stockings, injections, surgery, weight loss.
Outlook:	Good.
Prevention:	Raising legs when possible, support stockings, exercises, reduce weight.
Gravity rating 2:	See also phlebitis, embolus, thrombosis.

Common name:	**VERRUCA**
Alternate name(s):	Plantar warts.
Cause:	Possibly virus.
Early symptoms:	Small spot on sole of foot.
Course:	Pain and inflammation.
Complications:	Limping.
Treatment:	Curetting, cautery, liquid nitrogen, local applications.
Outlook:	Good.
Prevention:	Wearing slip-on shoes in gymnasia or swimming places.

Gravity rating 0

VITAMIN DEFICIENCY

Severe vitamin deficiency is now uncommon in developed countries because of improved nutrition. But marginal and occasionally serious deficiencies may occur because of prolonged illness and malnutrition in old age, alcoholism and drug abuse. The principle

VITAMIN	NATURAL SOURCE
A Retinol	Vegetables, dairy products, eggs, carrots, liver.
B1 Thiamine	Yeast, liver, meat, eggs, vegetables.
B2 Riboflavine	Green vegetables, lean meat, liver, eggs, cheese.
B3 Nicotinic acid	Yeast, liver, eggs, kidney, whole grain, cheese.
B5 Pantothenoic acid	Beans, egg yolk, liver, oranges, peanuts, wheat germ.
B6 Pyridoxine	Green vegetables, yeast, fish, prunes, raisins, soya, milk.

symptoms are listed on the next few pages. Treatment consists of improving the diet and if necessary giving the appropriate vitamin in concentrated form either by mouth or by injection.

EARLY SYMPTOMS	LATE SYMPTOMS
Night blindness, dry skin.	Dental decay, growth delay, infections.
Neuritis, fluid retention, fatigue, pins & needles.	Beriberi, heart failure.
Ulcers in angle of mouth, dizziness.	Black tongue, insomnia, scaly skin.
Poor appetite, nausea, peptic ulcers.	Pellagra, depression, dermatitis, diarrhoea.

Sometimes allergy, cramps, excess fatigue, insomnia.

Possibly a factor in neuritis.

VITAMIN	NATURAL SOURCE
B9 Folic acid	Liver, kidney, meat, fruits, yeast.
B12 Cyanocobalamin	Animal products, dairy products, yeast.
C Ascorbic acid	Green vegetables, citrus fruit, cooking may destroy.
D Cholecalciferol	Fish oils, eggs, sunlight, butter.
E Tocopherol	Vegetable oils, egg yolk, cereals, nuts.
K Menadione	Green vegetables, sea weed, liver, eggs, potatoes.

See also neuritis, pellagra, osteomalacia, scurvy, ricket

EARLY SYMPTOMS	LATE SYMPTOMS
Poor appetite, irritability, fatigue.	Anaemia, nerve degeneration.
Poor appetite, irritability, fatigue.	Anaemia, nerve degeneration.
Soft gums, bleeding, bruising, fatigue.	Anaemia, scurvy.
Dental caries, infections.	Rickets, osteomalacia.
	May be involved in sex organ and other dysfunctions.
	Defective blood clotting.

Common name: **WARTS**
Alternate name(s): Papillomata, benign skin tumours.
Cause: Probably virus infection.
Early symptoms: Small skin lumps becoming larger.
Course: Spread.
Complications: Infection.
Treatment: Local applications, cautery, freezing, curetting.
Outlook: Good.
Prevention: Personal cleanliness.
Gravity rating 0

Common name: **WHIPLASH**
Alternate name(s): Neck injury, torn intervertebral ligaments.
Cause: Violent backward and forward movement, often as a result of a rear end collison in car.
Early symptoms: Pain, stiffness, headache.
Course: Pain radiates to arms, giddiness.
Complications: Fracture, permanent disability, neurosis, depression.
Treatment: Immobilisation in collar, pain relief, muscle relaxants, physiotherapy, surgery.
Outlook: Fair.
Prevention: Careful driving, head rest in car, seat belts.
Gravity rating 3: See also slipped disc.

Common name:	**WHOOPING COUGH**
Alternate name(s):	Pertussis.
Cause:	Infection with whooping cough germ.
Early symptoms:	Cough, slight temperature.
Course:	Spasmodic cough with vomiting.
Complications:	Pneumonia, chronic lung infection, malnutrition.
Treatment:	Antibiotics, cough sedatives.
Outlook:	Good.
Prevention:	Vaccination, avoid contact with patient.

Gravity rating 2

GLOSSARY OF COMMON MEDICAL TERMS

Acute	Describing a disease or symptom of sudden onset and brief duration
Antacids	Drugs neutralising stomach acids
Anti–histamines	Drugs neutralising histamine, a factor in allergic reactions
Apnoea	Temporary cessation of breathing
Benign	A non-cancerous tumour. Any disorder without serious effects
Carbohydrates	Foods of the sugar and starch groups
Catheter	A tube passed into any body cavity to drain off fluid. Usually refers to the urinary bladder
Chemotherapy Treatment with chemicals	Usually refers to use of anti-infective and anti-cancer drugs
Chronic	Referring to a disease of long duration and slow progress
Congenital	Present at birth
Cryosurgery	Use of extreme cold to destroy diseased tissue
Curettage	Removal of diseased tissue by scraping with a sharp spoon shaped instrument
Cytotoxic	Describes drugs which destroy or damage diseased or normal cells

Dehydration	Severe reduction of water in tissues
Delusion	An irrationally held belief such as one of persecution or severe illness
Dialysis	Removal of poisons or other unwanted substances from the body by the use of an artificial kidney
Diuretics	Drugs to increase urine flow
Dysphagia	Difficult or painful swallowing
Dyspnoea	Distressed breathing
Dysuria	Difficulty or pain passing water
Enema	Fluid introduced into the lower bowel to remove faeces or for other purposes
Expectorant	Drug used to help removal of thick, sticky phlegm
Fallopian Tubes	Fine tubes through which eggs travel from the ovaries to the womb
Gangrene	Death of any tissue due to defective blood supply
Gastric	Referring to the stomach whether healthy or diseased
Genetic	Inherited
Gluten	A protein mixture present in wheat and rye
Halitosis	Foul breath
Hallucination	Seeing or hearing something which is not in fact present
Hereditary	Transmitted from parent(s) to child(ren)

Hormones   Substances produced by glands, such as the thyroid, which are carried in the blood stream and affect body functions

Hysterectomy   Surgical removal of the womb

Illusion   Faulty perception or interpretation of something which is present

Incontinence   Inability to control passage of urine or faeces

Infarct   Death of tissue due to blockage of an artery

Lachrimation   Excessive production of tears

Malaise   General feeling of being out-of-sorts

Malignancy   Growth which spreads to distant parts of the body

Metabolism   Chemical and physical changes in the body essential for normal function

Metastasis   Spread of a malignant tumour to another part of the body

Necrotic   Dead and decaying

Neoplasm   Abnormal growth of tissue

Neurosis   A mental illness in which the individual's behaviour or thought processes cause him or her distress or suffering

Oedema   Excessive accumulation of fluid in body tissues (dropsy)

Placebo	A medicine without active ingredients in which a patient has faith
Psychosis	A mental illness in which the patient loses touch with reality
Pus	Thick liquid in an infected area. Contains dead and living cells, bacteria and necrotic tissue
Secondary	Either an infection complicating some normally non-infective condition or a growth which has spread to some distant part of the body
Steroids	Anti-inflammatory drugs of the cortisone family
Suppositories	Medications introduced into the rectum or vagina
Symptomatic	Treatment aimed at relief of symptoms rather than cure
Syndrome	A combination of symptoms and signs making up a definite disorder
Ulcer	A break in the skin or mucous membrane
Vaccination	Technique for producing immunity to a disease by giving small amounts of infective material to stimulate the body's defences
Virus	A minute organism too small to be seen with an optical microscope and only capable of developing in living tissue